RED DEVIL

ZLATAN
IBRAHIMOVIĆ

COMING SOON

Paul Pogba: Pogboom

Ryan Giggs: Wing Wizard

Andrés Iniesta: The Illusionist

Cover illustration by Dan Leydon.
To learn more about Dan visit danleydon.com
To purchase his artwork visit etsy.com/shop/footynews
Or just follow him on Twitter @danleydon

RED DEVIL

ZLATAN
IBRAHIMOVIĆ

MATT AND TOM OLDFIELD

DINO

Published by Dino Books
an imprint of John Blake Publishing Ltd
3 Bramber Court, 2 Bramber Road,
London W14 9PB, England

www.johnblakepublishing.co.uk

www.facebook.com/johnblakebooks f
twitter.com/jblakebooks t

First published in paperback in 2017

ISBN: 978 1 78 606 217 8

British Library Cataloguing-in-Publication Data:

A catalogue record for this book is available from the British Library.

Design by www.envydesign.co.uk
Cover illustration by Dan Leydon
Background image: Shutterstock

Printed in Great Britain by CPI Group (UK) Ltd

1 3 5 7 9 10 8 6 4 2

Papers used by John Blake Publishing are natural, recyclable products made from
wood grown in sustainable forests. The manufacturing processes conform to the
environmental regulations of the country of origin.

Every attempt has been made to contact the relevant copyright-holders, but some
were unobtainable. We would be grateful if the appropriate people could contact us.

For Noah and the future Oldfields to come

Looking forward to reading this book together

TABLE OF CONTENTS

ACKNOWLEDGEMENTS

First of all, I'd like to thank John Blake Publishing –
and particularly my editor James Hodgkinson – for
giving me the opportunity to work on these books
and for supporting me throughout. Writing stories for
the next generation of football fans is both an honour
and a pleasure.

I wouldn't be doing this if it wasn't for Tom. I owe
him so much and I'm very grateful for his belief in
me as an author. I feel like Robin setting out on a
solo career after a great partnership with Batman. I
hope I do him (Tom, not Batman) justice with these
new books.

Next up, I want to thank my friends for keeping
me sane during long hours in front of the laptop.

Pang, Will, Mills, Doug, John, Charlie – the laughs and the cups of coffee are always appreciated.

I've already thanked my brother but I'm also very grateful to the rest of my family, especially Melissa, Noah and of course Mum and Dad. To my parents, I owe my biggest passions: football and books. They're a real inspiration for everything I do.

Finally, I couldn't have done this without Iona's encouragement and understanding during long, work-filled weekends. Much love to you.

CHAPTER 1

CHAMPION OF FRANCE

Paris Saint-Germain needed one more win to become Champions of France for the first time in nearly twenty years. The younger players were very nervous but luckily, they had a leader who knew all about pressure.

'Do you believe in me?' Zlatan asked his manager, Carlo Ancelotti, in front of the whole team in the dressing room before kick-off.

'Of course,' Ancelotti replied. Zlatan was the top scorer in the league and was always saving the day for PSG with his goals.

'Then you can relax!' Zlatan said. 'We will win this title, I promise.'

Ever since he was a small kid growing up in the tough Rosengård district of Malmö in Sweden, Zlatan had always had great self-belief. He had to believe that he was the best in order to become the best. From the great boxer Muhammad Ali, he had learnt to 'talk the talk' but also 'walk the walk'. If Zlatan said that PSG would win the league, then he would make sure it happened.

PSG were playing away at title rivals Lyon. The Lyon players and fans were desperate to stop Zlatan and his teammates from winning the league in their stadium. It wasn't easy to stop Zlatan, though. In fact, it was impossible. He was tall, quick, strong, skilful and good at shooting – he had it all. Early in the match, he had a shot stopped on the goal-line by a defender.

'Keep going!' he shouted to his teammates. 'The goal will come!'

In the second half, Zlatan got the ball and ran forward. He passed to midfielder Thiago Motta and the Lyon defenders expected the one-two. Zlatan was the danger man and so they ran towards him and left lots of space for his strike partner Jérémy Ménez. Thiago passed to Jérémy instead and he shot into the bottom corner.

Gooooooooooaaaaaaaaaaaaaaaaaaalllllllllllll llll!!!!!!!!!!!!!!

It was such a relief to be winning. The PSG players hugged each other but they knew it wasn't over yet. Zlatan knew he couldn't think too much about his crucial assist – he had to make sure that they all stayed focused.

'We've only got half an hour to go, guys – concentrate!'

The PSG players always listened to their star striker. At the final whistle, they jumped for joy. Zlatan had done what he had promised at the start of the season – he had helped PSG to win the league. The whole team joined together and danced around the pitch.

Championes, Championes, Olé Olé Olé!

Then they ran towards the PSG fans to clap them for all of their support during the season. Zlatan never forgot how lucky he was to be playing the sport that he loved in front of thousands of people who loved him. He was so pleased to have won the trophy for the supporters. The players threw their shirts into the crowd and put on T-shirts that read

'Paris are Champions'. Even Ancelotti put the T-shirt on over his smart suit.

With the TV cameras watching, Zlatan roared like a lion. It was his tenth league title in only twelve years but he never got tired of winning. It was the best feeling in the world. It was the reason why he kept working so hard every day on the training ground, learning new tricks and improving his skills. He hated losing and he loved trophies. It had been one of his best seasons ever. He was the Ligue 1 top goalscorer and the Player of the Year too.

'We've won the league again!' he shouted to Maxwell. They were best friends and they had played together at Ajax, Inter Milan, Barcelona and PSG. At four different clubs in Holland, Italy, Spain and now France, they had won trophy after trophy.

'Do you remember when I first joined you at Ajax and I didn't have any money?' Zlatan said with his arm around his friend's shoulder.

Maxwell laughed. 'Yes, I had to make you dinner every night. You were a really arrogant young kid back then – you had so many enemies!'

Zlatan had come a very long way from the small, angry street footballer who lived in a dangerous part of Malmö. He had always had lots of talent but there were many important lessons that he needed to learn to become a superstar.

'I was different and they didn't like that,' was Zlatan's defence. It had taken a while for him to work out how to make the most of his special character on the pitch.

During his time at Ajax, he had begun to control his temper. He became more of a team player and he focused on scoring goals rather than just showing off his tricks. Now, at PSG and aged thirty, he was a tall, skilful, world-class striker and a leader on the pitch. He had become Sweden's top goalscorer and the most expensive player of all time. Everyone knew his name.

Zlatan! Zlatan! Zlatan!

It had been a journey full of drama and adventure and Zlatan had enjoyed every minute of it. Maxwell, Mino, Mourinho, Helena, his dad – there were so many people who had helped him to achieve his dreams.

'You've grown up a lot since then,' Maxwell admitted.

'I know, but I'm still the kid from Rosengård!' Zlatan replied with a big smile on his face.

CHAPTER 2

ROSENGÅRD

'Zlatan!' Jurka shouted out into the cold night air.
'Zlatan!'

She stood at the front door to the flat and waited
to hear the sound of her son's BMX bike whizzing
through the estate. Zlatan was too young to be out
playing at night, especially in an area like Rosengård.
Not many of the streetlights worked and there were
lots of broken windows in the tall tower blocks.
There was always trouble in the neighbourhood and
Jurka never stopped worrying about her children. But
Zlatan didn't like to listen to his mother or anyone
else; he already thought he could look after himself.

'Don't worry, I'll be fine!' he would say with a
smile as he rode off to meet up with his friends.

Zlatan was small for his age but he had a lot of self-confidence.

Jurka worked very hard as a cleaner to earn enough money for her family but it meant that she was rarely at home to keep an eye on them. When she wasn't there, Jurka tried to make sure that the kids had dinner at her sister's house, or at their friends' homes. Otherwise, they roamed the streets and ate instant noodles and tomato sauce for dinner.

It wasn't a healthy way to grow up but Jurka couldn't afford anything better. She loved her children but she had to be strict with them. Her daughter Sanela was a good girl but Jurka had to hope and trust that Zlatan was behaving himself.

'Sorry Mum!' Zlatan shouted as he rushed up the four flights of dirty stairs to the flat. He was starving.

'Where have you been?' Jurka asked straightaway.

'Just around the estate,' he replied, still out of breath. 'We played a long game of football. My team won, of course!'

Jurka nodded; she was happy to hear that Zlatan was playing football. Her son had so much energy to burn and sport kept him out of trouble too.

'What's for dinner?' Zlatan asked, walking into the kitchen.

'You can cook for yourself!' Sanela said, giving him a playful slap. 'But wash yourself first – you stink!'

'Hey, that's not fair!'

'Why should we get the food ready, while you're out having fun?'

'Go and argue in the other room!' Jurka told her children, pushing them out of the kitchen. She was tired after a long day and there was always so much noise in her home. She needed a bit of peace and quiet.

There was never any space in the flat, however. Zlatan's two half-sisters lived there too, as well as his younger half-brother Keki.

'What's new?' Zlatan asked as he sat down in front of the TV after a quick shower.

'Nothing,' was Keki's one word response. He didn't even look up.

'Why won't you talk to me?' Zlatan said, standing in front of the screen to get his half-brother's attention. He wanted to look after Keki and make sure he wasn't getting involved in anything bad. It was so easy to get in trouble in Rosengård. Things were always being stolen and there were lots of fights on the estate.

'Leave me alone and get out of the way!'

Zlatan stormed out of the room; he was only trying to help his brother. There was a lot of anger in their home and he wasn't always to blame. Doors were always slamming and their mother was often crying. As they ate dinner, there was more fighting and more drama. Life was never easy.

'Are you seeing your father this weekend?' Jurka asked Zlatan and Sanela when everything had calmed down a little.

The two of them nodded. Sanela didn't mind but Zlatan couldn't wait to see his dad. Things were always more fun with him. Šefik always took them out for pizza and coke, or burgers and ice cream. One day, he had even bought them brand new Nike Air Max trainers: green for Zlatan and pink for Sanela. It was the best present Zlatan had ever received.

'Wow, these are the coolest shoes ever!' he said with a big smile on his face.

He was really excited to show them off to his

friends. They would be so jealous. In Rosengård,
there were kids from lots of different countries:
not only Sweden but also Somalia, Turkey, Poland,
Serbia, Croatia, Slovenia – and Bosnia, where
Zlatan's dad Šefik hailed from. They all had different
cultures and spoke different languages but they had
one thing in common; they all wanted to be the best
but more importantly they wanted to look the best.
Style, or 'swagger', was very important.

'Okay, well tidy up the living room before you go,'
Jurka told them. 'This place is always such a mess.'

CHAPTER 3

MUHAMMAD ALI

'Dad, is there anything to eat?' Zlatan shouted through from the kitchen. The fridge was empty as usual, apart from a pint of milk.

'There's a loaf of bread in the cupboard,' Šefik replied from his armchair.

Zlatan sighed; it would have to do. He had moved in with his dad and Sanela was living with their mum. It wasn't perfect, especially when Zlatan was hungry. He was small and weak and without a good diet he would never grow up to be big and strong like his heroes on TV.

'Come and watch this with me,' Šefik said, patting the chair next to him. Zlatan's dad didn't like Swedish culture; instead, he listened to loud

Yugoslavian folk music and watched old films. Bruce
Lee and Jackie Chan martial arts movies were usually
his favourites but this particular film was different.

'Your uncle Sapko was a brilliant boxer,' Šefik
began and Zlatan listened carefully, as his father
rarely spoke about his old life in Bosnia. 'He was
famous back home and he was selected for the
Yugoslavian national team. Then one day, when he
was only twenty-three, he drowned in the river. It
was the worst time of my life but ever since then,
I've loved watching boxing. And this guy is the best
of all time.'

Zlatan watched as Muhammad Ali beat George
Foreman in the famous fight called 'The Rumble in
the Jungle'. As Ali won in the eighth round, Zlatan
cheered. It was the best match he had ever seen
and Ali was his new favourite boxer. He wasn't the
biggest but he was really quick and really cool. He
had lots of 'swagger'.

Before the match, Ali boasted to the media, saying
things like: 'I'm so fast that last night I turned off
the light switch in my hotel room and got into bed
before the room was dark.' It was very funny but Ali

could walk the walk as well as talk the talk. He had excellent technique, as he danced around the ring, ducking punches until the time was right to strike back.

'That all you got, George?' Ali said again and again during the fight. 'That all you got?'

Zlatan loved every second of it. He had a new hero.

*　*　*

'I am the greatest!' Zlatan shouted as he ran into the playground. It was break-time at Varner Rydén School and that meant only one thing – football.

Zlatan wasn't the best footballer at school but he worked really hard to improve his technique. Like Ali, he was determined to become a legend, no matter what it took. Sometimes, his determination made him really angry. He tried to stay calm on the pitch but often he screamed at his teammates if they made a bad pass, or he made bad fouls on purpose.

'Chill out, Zlatan!' his friends would say and he would sit in the corner and take deep breaths until he was ready to play again. He tried to control his temper but there was real fire in his belly. On the football pitch, he let out all of his frustration about his family life.

Zlatan often played football after school until it was too dark to see the ball. Then he would go to his mum's house in search of food and a catch-up with Sanela and Keki. On the walk home to his dad's house, Zlatan had to be as brave as Muhammad Ali. The path was a very dangerous route at night – there were only a couple of dim streetlights and lots of bushes and alleyways – and Šefik had been badly injured during an attack.

'I am the greatest!' Zlatan would say to himself, his heart beating much faster than usual. If he ran fast enough, nothing bad could ever happen. When he reached the first lamppost, he thought, 'Right, only one more to go!'

Šefik taught Zlatan to be tough and always stand up for himself. This was one of his dad's main rules, along with: always try to do better, always do the right thing and never give up. He wasn't the most affectionate father but he did give Zlatan some very valuable lessons. One day, Šefik bought a new IKEA bed for his son.

'Would you like that delivered, sir?' the shop assistant asked him.

'Does that cost extra?' he replied. The shop assistant nodded.

Šefik couldn't afford the delivery charge and so he carried the mattress all the way home for mile after mile. Zlatan carried the legs but he couldn't keep up with his dad.

'Wait! Can we take a break?' he moaned.

'No!' his dad replied with sweat dripping down his face.

Zlatan rolled his eyes and kept going. Sometimes you had to make sacrifices to achieve your goals.

CHAPTER 4

SHOWING OFF

'Good morning,' the teacher said loudly. Zlatan had hoped to slip into class without her noticing. She didn't look happy. 'It's nice of you to join us but why are you so late?'

Zlatan looked up at the clock on the wall and then down at the floor. He had missed nearly an hour of school for the third time that week. He had run out of excuses and so he decided to be honest.

'Sorry, I missed my alarm,' he said, trying to look as innocent as possible.

'Well, I'll be having a chat with your parents about this,' his teacher replied. 'But for now, take a seat and open your books.'

Zlatan liked learning and he did well in exams

when he studied hard. But he found it very difficult
to sit still for more than a few minutes at a time.
In Maths, he usually got the right answers but that
wasn't enough.

'Well done Zlatan, but you need to explain how
you got to that answer,' his teacher would always say
but he wasn't interested in showing the workings.
Sometimes, it was assumed he was cheating but
he wasn't.

'Zlatan, pay attention!' the teacher shouted. He
was discussing football with one of his friends at the
back of the room. It was impossible to control Zlatan
when he was bored. Soon, he was throwing pencils
across the room.

'Right, go and stand outside, Zlatan!' the teacher
said after several warnings. Once the other children
were studying again, she came out to speak with him.

'I know you're not a bad kid,' she said and Zlatan
started to feel very guilty, 'but you need to behave
in my class. The other kids want to learn and you're
stopping them by acting like a fool. Do you really
hate school?'

Zlatan shook his head.

'Then show me that you can behave, or I'll have to speak to the headmaster.'

Šefik moved home quite a few times, meaning that with each house move, Zlatan had to move to a new school. It was hard to get used to each new environment and make new friends. Instead, his constant friends were his teammates and opponents in the daily football matches on the estate. They were long, tough battles and Zlatan loved them. The boys didn't wear brand new football kits to play; instead, they wore their normal clothes and old trainers. They went home with holes in the knees of their jeans, cuts on their elbows and smiles on their faces. It was the best part of every day.

'What do you mean I can't play?' Zlatan shouted. He was getting very angry. He had run all the way from school to make sure that he didn't miss the start of the game. There was nothing he hated more than being left out. He was good enough to play.

'We've got enough players today and you're too small,' the leader told him, but Zlatan could see that he was a bit scared of him. Zlatan was small like a mouse but he had the heart of a lion.

'You guys are rubbish,' he replied. 'I'm the best player here!'

'Okay fine – prove it!' the boy said eventually.

Zlatan could talk the talk but could he walk the walk? When they let him play, he had to show them that he was worth it. And it wasn't just about scoring goals; it was about scoring *great* goals. In street football, the kids cheered loudest for the coolest tricks.

For the first few minutes, his teammates wouldn't pass the ball to him. Zlatan kept shouting for it but they took a shot instead or passed to someone else. He was the outsider and they didn't trust him yet. Finally, Zlatan made a good tackle and won the ball for himself. He ran forward, nutmegged one defender, flicked it past the next and then smashed a shot past the goalkeeper. Zlatan didn't celebrate; he was too cool for that. He didn't even smile.

Oooooooooooooohhhhhh...

'Nice goal!' one of his teammates said, giving him a high-five. He was part of the group now.

For Zlatan, football was a great escape from Rosengård, from hunger, crime and family arguments. On the pitch, he forgot about everything

and focused on his ball control and his skills. The
pitch was small, so his feet had to be quick in
confined spaces. Zlatan wouldn't let his size stop
him; nothing could stop him. He loved trying new
skills, inventing crazy moves in his head that he
knew the other kids would enjoy. He was improving
all the time because he was determined to be
the best.

'I can score much better goals!' he told his
teammates with his usual confidence. He got the
ball and weaved through three opponents. With just
the goalkeeper to beat, Zlatan flicked the ball up,
did a couple of keepy-uppies and volleyed the ball
powerfully past him. Again, Zlatan didn't celebrate;
he just turned around as if it was nothing.

Eeeeeeeeeeeeeyyyyyyyyy...

The next time the ball came to him, lots of players
surrounded him. He pretended to run forward but
instead played a cool 'no-look' pass across to his
teammate.

Oooooooooooooohhhhhh...

He could tell that the other kids were starting to
respect him now.

As he rushed off to his mum's house for dinner, his teammates called out to him. 'So we'll see you same time tomorrow, Zlatan?'

He smiled and shrugged. 'We'll see.'

CHAPTER 5

BALKAN BRILLIANCE

'Pass the ball!' the coach shouted again and again but Zlatan didn't listen. All he wanted to do was dribble and perform the skills that he had learnt on the estate. It was a bit more difficult on this gravel pitch but he liked a challenge. The other young players in the Malmö Ball and Sporting Association (MBI) weren't happy.

'Coach, this isn't fun,' they protested. 'He's not a team player!'

The parents complained too and so the coach had a word with Zlatan.

'They're just jealous because I'm better than them,' was his quick reply. He was used to defending himself.

'Football isn't about showing off,' the coach said. 'It's about passing and playing together as a team.'

Zlatan shook his head and kicked the ball away angrily. He was tired of being different from the other Swedish kids.

'Well, if you don't want to play, you can go home!' the coach shouted. He had had enough.

Zlatan stormed off home. When he told his dad about what had happened, Šefik just said, 'Don't worry, we'll find you another club to play for.'

At the FBK Balkan club, Zlatan felt more at home. The coach let the boy play the way he wanted to play but he also criticised him when appropriate. Zlatan was one of the best but at first, he played as a goalkeeper.

'The other keeper isn't good enough, so I'll take over,' he told the coach. Zlatan believed he could do anything.

After a few games, however, he got bored. He was letting in lots of goals and he missed playing outfield with the ball at his feet. Perhaps Zlatan wasn't good at *everything*.

'Coach, I want to play up front instead,' Zlatan said and straightaway, he started to score goals.

Sometimes, though, Zlatan was as late for football as he was for school. One day, the game was about to start and he still wasn't there. The coach and the other players were furious.

'Who does he think he is?'

'It's not fair – the rest of us always turn up on time.'

Zlatan arrived right at the last minute and won the game for them. The FBK Balkan club couldn't cope without him. But in the next game, the coach put him on the bench. By half-time, they were losing 4–0.

'It's stupid leaving me out!' he told the coach.

'If you calm down, Zlatan, I'll bring you on soon.'

In the second half, Zlatan was so determined that he scored eight goals. As he called for the ball, he was already thinking about his next skilful display. He looked at where the defenders were and in his head he pictured what he would do to beat them. On the estate, he had learnt how to do amazing things in small spaces. On a bigger pitch, his approach worked a treat.

'Zlatan, you're a very good player but you have to behave yourself,' the coach told him at the end of the match. 'And you have to learn to control your temper.'

When things weren't going well, Zlatan got angry and kicked his opponents. The referees knew all about him and often sent him off.

'Not again!' the coach would say as Zlatan stormed off home after another red card.

Despite being Balkan's star player, Zlatan still preferred the matches on the estate. Every night, the courtyard there was the most important place in the world. Zlatan felt more comfortable and free when he played with street rules. To him, football was all about showing off your skills. Passing and defending were boring. It was more fun to dribble past players and do cool tricks.

As he got older and better, Zlatan liked to challenge the younger kids.

'Right, the first person to get the ball off me, gets a chocolate bar!' he said, standing in the middle of the pitch. Sometimes there were ten of them trying to tackle him but Zlatan was so good with the ball at his

feet. Slowly the youngsters gave up and went home:
'It's impossible!'

Zlatan travelled to all of his matches on his bike.
From a very young age, he had learnt to look after
himself. Other players had their parents cheering
them on but Šefik was usually too busy working.
He couldn't watch his son's matches but he knew
that he had lots of talent. Zlatan loved talking to him
about football.

One day, Šefik said, 'Son, I think you need a new
challenge. I think it's time to play for a bigger club.'

Zlatan liked the sound of that but he didn't know
much about Swedish football clubs. 'Who can I play
for?'

'Malmö FF,' his dad replied.

CHAPTER 6

ZLATAN THE BRAZILIAN

'Welcome to the team,' Nils said when Zlatan turned up for his training session. The Malmö youth coach had heard about this great raw talent and he was excited about working with him.

But from day one, Zlatan felt like an outsider amongst all of the polite Swedish kids. He was the only one there from the Rosengård estate. He talked differently, his parents didn't come to watch him play and he didn't live in a big house. The others all had the best new Adidas football boots, whereas he had bought the cheapest pair at the local supermarket.

'We're going to go and get pizza,' his teammates said after one practice. 'Do you want to come?'

It was a really kind offer but Zlatan didn't have enough money to join them. Sometimes he hated being different, the odd one out. He wished that he could buy expensive clothes and cars to fit in. But living with his dad, he often didn't have enough money to buy bread.

'The fridge is empty again!' he called out when he got home from practice. His dad was asleep in his chair in front of the TV. 'One day when I'm a professional footballer,' Zlatan said to himself, 'I won't have to worry about having enough food.'

On the pitch, he was an outsider too.

'What are you doing?' Zlatan shouted at one of his teammates. The boy looked really shocked but that was just how Zlatan always talked to his friends on the estate. 'Pass me the ball!'

Again, the parents complained about Malmö's new young player. He was too aggressive and he dribbled too much. Their sons were scared of him. One day, they presented a big petition to the manager, asking for Zlatan to be kicked out of the team. But the manager took one look and ripped it up.

'Give Zlatan a chance,' he told the parents. 'He's a

brilliant player and he just needs time to adapt to this kind of football.'

Zlatan was sorry that he had upset people. He was trying to improve his behaviour but it wasn't easy to change.

'I'll work harder,' he promised Nils. 'I'll train harder, so that I'm better than everyone else.'

His teammates loved the Swedish national team players but Zlatan had never heard of any of them. He only knew the Brazilians because they performed lots of cool skills. In their yellow shirts and blue shorts, they played like they were having fun. Like Zlatan, they were entertainers – Bebeto and Romário were his favourites. It was 1994, and on the estate, they would watch Brazil's World Cup matches on TV and then go out and copy what they had seen.

In the World Cup's group stage, Sweden and Brazil played each other.

'We're going to beat you!' his Malmö teammates told Zlatan.

'No chance!' he replied.

Kennet Andersson put Sweden ahead but then Romário dribbled through their defence and scored a great goal. The game finished 1–1 and everyone was satisfied.

'Brazil are going to win the World Cup, though!' Zlatan said with his usual confidence. In training, he always liked to add his own special touch to the skills he had seen on TV and soon the Malmö players were doing the same.

'Did you see Bebeto's flick? How did he do that?'

'That goal celebration was brilliant. Let's do something like that next time we score!'

Eventually, everyone accepted Zlatan. He wasn't a bad kid; he was just different in a very special way. No-one knew what he would do next and that made it very hard for his opponents to defend against him. The team was doing well and he was a key part of their success. The star of the Malmö team at this point was called Tony, and Zlatan learnt lots from playing with him. They became really good friends and did everything together.

'My dad's got tickets for the Trelleborgs match against Blackburn,' Tony said excitedly one day. 'Do you want to come?'

Zlatan had only ever seen Malmö play and this was a chance to see a big UEFA Cup game. 'Yes please!'

he said. Tony's dad drove them to the match and on the way Tony talked about Blackburn's best player.

'I can't wait to see Alan Shearer play – he's amazing. Last season he scored thirty-one goals in England!'

Zlatan didn't know anything about these players – if they weren't Brazilian, he didn't care. 'Do they have anyone that can do lots of cool skills?' he asked.

'Not really,' Tony replied. 'One day, you'll learn that there's more to football than tricks!'

Zlatan didn't agree but it was a really exciting match. In the first leg in England, Trelleborgs had achieved a shock 1–0 win. Lots of Blackburn fans travelled to Sweden for the second leg and the atmosphere was great.

Chris Sutton scored to make it 1–1 and the Trelleborgs fans feared that they would lose. But in the second half, Joachim Karlsson scored a brilliant goal. Zlatan cheered loudly along with all of the Trelleborgs supporters.

'You're a fan now, are you?' Tony asked. He was supporting Blackburn because of his hero, Alan Shearer.

'Yes, I'm Swedish!' Zlatan laughed.

With seven minutes to go, Shearer headed the ball into the net. Blackburn were level again but not for long. Karlsson scored again and the stadium went wild. Trelleborgs had beaten one of the biggest clubs in Britain.

'How exciting was that?' Tony said with a big grin on his face as they walked out of the stadium and back to the car.

Zlatan nodded. He was thinking about his own football dreams. It would be incredible to play in big European matches in front of thousands of fans, plus lots of TV cameras too. He pictured himself dribbling past defenders like Romário.

'I still prefer the Brazilians!' he said.

CHAPTER 7

RONALDO VS SHEARER

'Are you happy here?' the Malmö youth manager asked Zlatan one day.

Zlatan took a minute to think and then nodded slowly. 'I guess so.'

'That's good because you're a great young player and we don't want to lose you,' the manager said with a friendly smile. 'Bring your dad along next week and you can sign a youth contract with us.'

Zlatan's face lit up. He was going to earn money by playing football. It was so exciting and it made him even more determined to work hard and be the best. He practised controlling the ball for hours and hours until he could do it really quickly and with only one or two touches.

'You've got incredible technique,' Tony told him as they did some extra training together one day. Zlatan loved to be praised, especially by his best friend. 'But you have to learn when to dribble, when to shoot and when to just pass.'

Zlatan didn't always listen to instructions and he still shouted at his teammates when they made mistakes. But he was certainly becoming more of a team player. He was learning from his mistakes and he was discovering a great deal about football tactics. They were a good group of boys and if he passed to them, he knew he would get the ball back to score. It was always fun to win.

When he was fourteen years old, Zlatan found a new hero. He still loved Muhammad Ali's swagger but there was a new Brazilian superstar who played football with the kind of style that he loved. His name was Ronaldo.

'Tony, come and look at this!' Zlatan shouted as they sat together in an internet café near the Malmö training ground. They watched video after video of the Brazilian's best goals. There were so many of them. 'He's strong, he's quick, he's skilful and he's a goalscorer – he's incredible!'

'He's good but I prefer Alan Shearer,' Tony said.

'You don't know anything!' Zlatan replied. 'Have you ever seen him dribble? He doesn't have any skills – he's boring!'

The two boys never agreed about anything – it was much more fun to argue for hours and hours.

Zlatan put up posters of Ronaldo in his bedroom and he started doing lots of step-overs and dancing down the pitch like his idol. Zlatan was getting taller and taller and it was harder to dribble with long legs. The skills didn't always work and sometimes the manager got angry at him for losing the ball.

'Just shoot!' the parents on the touchline screamed to him.

But Zlatan never gave up. Swedish footballers usually didn't show off but he didn't want to be a typical Swedish player. He wanted to entertain the world like his heroes.

'I'm not interested in being average,' he told Tony. 'I'm only interested in being the best!'

At secondary school, Zlatan tried to look as cool as possible but it was like Malmö all over again. He wore his best Adidas tracksuits but the rich kids wore Ralph Lauren jumpers. He was different – the kid from Rosengård. He bought new jeans and polo shirts but he still didn't really fit in.

Also, Zlatan didn't really like studying. He was clever but he could never pay attention for long. As the teacher talked, he would start thinking about football. What new tricks could he do in training? If he tried that, what would the defender do? His mind played videos of him dribbling at defenders, and he couldn't wait to get outside and play. When he talked to his classmates or played practical jokes, he got in lots of trouble.

'You've had three warnings now – get out of my class!' his Italian teacher shouted.

Zlatan was sorry but he loved to act cool. 'I don't care,' he said as he walked out. 'I'll learn all of this when I'm a professional in Italy!'

Football was Zlatan's big chance to make a good life for himself. He watched his friends from the estate getting involved in crime and drinking alcohol. Zlatan didn't want that.

'I've made some stupid mistakes but I know I can

achieve great things,' he told his dad as they watched a film together one night.

'I believe in you, son,' Šefik said. 'If you work hard and don't take no for an answer, you'll make it to the top.'

Zlatan was pleased to hear his dad say that. 'But do you think I can be a professional footballer?'

'Yes, I do. But if it doesn't work out, I think you should become a lawyer.'

'Dad, that's impossible! The teachers at school hate me,' Zlatan replied. No, it would have to be football.

CHAPTER 8

MAKE OR BREAK

'Don't worry, you'll get your chance,' Tony reassured him, as they warmed up before a match.

For the first time, Zlatan was having second thoughts about playing football. He was fifteen years old and suddenly he was sitting on the bench for the Malmö youth team. When he did come on, he usually scored goals but his footballing idol Ronaldo was never a substitute. If Zlatan couldn't get into the starting eleven of the Malmö youth team, what chance did he have of becoming a top professional? Perhaps it was time to think about getting a job instead.

'I could go and work at the docks,' Zlatan suggested to his dad but Šefik didn't like that idea.

'Don't give up just because you're different,' he told his son. 'You just have to work even harder to prove yourself.'

Zlatan knew that he was good enough but he needed a coach that believed in him. He had grown a lot in the last few years and he was now taller than most defenders. His close control was brilliant and he often did magical things that no-one expected. But he was still a raw talent and sometimes he had really bad games where none of his skills worked. He wasn't consistent and that was a big problem.

Tony was starting to train with the senior squad but there was no way they'd want Zlatan. He knew what everyone said about him:

'That Zlatan kid has got great technique but he's too arrogant.'

'He's got everything except the ability to listen.'

Malmö were really struggling. They were near the bottom of the top Swedish league and they didn't have any money to buy new players. They would have to rely on their youth team, but Zlatan was sure that he could save them.

'If they'd just give me a chance, I'd be amazing!'

he told Tony. Together, they could be the future of
the club.

The problem was that Malmö didn't want a flashy
striker – they just needed someone who could
score lots of goals and play by the rules. That wasn't
Zlatan's way. When he finally got asked to train with
the senior squad, he refused to change. Most junior
players were quiet and respectful but not Zlatan. He
went in for lots of big tackles and tried to perform as
many skills as possible. He could tell that the older
players weren't impressed.

'Who does he think he is?'

'Why doesn't he just pass the ball? He's far too
cocky!'

Zlatan knew that Roland Andersson, the Malmö
coach, was watching and he hoped that he was
impressed by his talent. The other Swedish players
were all the same but he was unique, special.

Even so, the next week, Zlatan was back playing
for the Under-20s. He tried his best to catch the eye
of those in charge but it wasn't working.

'Guys like me don't have a chance,' he told
Tony one day. He didn't have the energy to keep

fighting. He was finished with football. It was time to move on.

His friend disagreed. 'Look, why don't you give it one more year and if you're still not playing for the senior team, you can stop?'

Zlatan thought about it for a while and decided that was a good plan. He was still only sixteen. After years in the Malmö youth team, he couldn't give up just yet. He really wanted to be a professional footballer.

'Okay, one more year!'

He wiped the sweat from his forehead and walked off the pitch. The Under-20s had won again and he was the hero with another couple of goals. He was pleased with his improvement, especially when it came to shooting. He had always had power but now he was much more accurate. As he moved towards the changing room, one of the Malmö coaches came over to him.

'Hi Zlatan, Roland Andersson wants to talk to you,' he said and led him towards the manager's office.

Zlatan was worried – what had he done wrong? He couldn't think of anything but the club always seemed to have something to complain about.

'Come in,' Andersson said in his loud, deep voice from behind the desk. He looked very serious and Zlatan could hear his heart beating fast as he sat down opposite him.

'I've been watching your performances for months and I think it's time,' Andersson said.

'Time for what?' Zlatan replied. Was he being kicked out of the club?

'It's time for you to move up from the kids to the big boys.'

'I don't understand.'

'Welcome to the first team,' Andersson said, shaking his hand.

Zlatan couldn't believe it. He had waited so long for this moment and now it was finally here. Zlatan usually tried to look as cool as possible but this wasn't a normal day. The best feeling in the world deserved his biggest smile.

Zlatan Ibrahimović, Malmö first team footballer. This was just the start.

CHAPTER 9

READY TO SHINE

'This run is so boring!' Zlatan said to Tony. The Malmö squad often ran 'The Mile' as a warm-up before training and Zlatan hated it. After a few kilometres, they were way behind the other players. 'Let's just get the bus instead.'

When they got off, they hid and waited for the rest of the team to run past. This was Zlatan's favourite part of the route because they went past his old school, where they had told him that he didn't have the right attitude to succeed. He was proving them wrong and he loved to run past alongside the famous Malmö players. It was also a great chance to impress the girls at school.

'They'll be so impressed when we run past,

looking really athletic in our club kits!' Zlatan said to Tony.

'Sure, but they still won't be interested in you!' Tony joked and Zlatan gave him a friendly slap.

The older players weren't very happy with the way the new youngsters behaved. They were supposed to be polite and carry all of the equipment, but Zlatan refused.

'I'm not their servant!' he complained. 'How can I respect them when they lose every game?'

Malmö were in danger of relegation for the first time in sixty-four years. That would be a disaster and Zlatan was determined to save the day. He worked extra hard in training but he still wasn't playing in the matches. When Tony scored on his debut, that made Zlatan even more impatient.

'If they don't give me a game soon, it'll be too late!' he told his dad.

Zlatan was on the bench for a very important match against Halmstad. Malmö needed at least one point to avoid relegation. There were a lot of nerves in the squad but Zlatan was calm. He just hoped that he would come on for his debut.

In the second-half, their star striker got injured and
Zlatan looked at his manager. Was this his chance
to shine? Roland Andersson brought on another
midfielder instead. Zlatan was really disappointed
but then their captain also got injured. Malmö were
losing 2–1 – they needed a goal.

'Zlatan, you're coming on,' Andersson told him.

Zlatan ran onto the pitch in front of 10,000 fans,
wearing the blue-and-white shirt for the very first
time. He couldn't wait to do something special.
Nothing could stop him now. In the first few
minutes, the ball came to Zlatan and he used his skill
to create a bit of space. His shot flew towards the
goal... but it hit the crossbar.

'Unlucky, mate!' Tony shouted to him.

'Next time,' Zlatan replied. He couldn't wait to
celebrate his first goal with all of the supporters.

In the last few minutes, Malmö won a penalty.
If they scored, they would stay in the top division.
It was a massive moment. Zlatan wanted to take it
but he knew they wouldn't let him on his debut.
But when no-one else was willing to take it, Tony
stepped up.

'Wow, you're a cocky kid!' Zlatan joked with him. 'You better score this.'

The other players looked away as Tony ran up to strike the ball. It was a good shot but the goalkeeper saved it. Tony fell to the floor. He could have been the hero but instead, he was the villain.

'Don't worry, you were brave to take the responsibility,' Zlatan said, putting an arm around his friend. But after that, Tony was dropped from the team and Zlatan began to play more games. He was young and exciting to watch. The fans loved him and soon they waited after matches to ask for his autograph.

'Zlatan, you're my hero!' they shouted.

It was an amazing feeling – it was like he was a real superstar already. Zlatan stayed until he had signed every last autograph. Their passion inspired him to do more and more tricks. Even if Malmö were relegated, he didn't want to disappoint the youngsters. Andersson told the media that Zlatan was 'a diamond in the rough'. That made him really happy.

Everything was going so well for Zlatan. One day, during a team training session, he spotted a man watching from a distance. It was strange because fans didn't normally turn up at practice. Zlatan tried to entertain him with his full range of tricks. The man moved a little closer and suddenly he realised who it was.

'Dad!' he shouted and waved.

It was one of the first times that Šefik had ever watched him play. Zlatan was so happy to see him. It was a dream come true. After so many years without a parent on the sidelines, now he had his dad there, cheering him on.

'Well played, son,' Šefik said when they met up after the session. As Zlatan introduced his dad to his teammates, he felt so proud. With his support, Zlatan was ready to shine.

CHAPTER 10

REMEMBER
THE NAME

Rune Smith was a very busy sports journalist but he was always interested when Hasse Borg called. The Malmö sporting director only got in touch when he had big news.

'Rune, we've got a young player here who you'll love,' Hasse said on the phone. 'Honestly, what he does is magic. I've never seen anyone play like him.'

Rune was very excited. Sweden had lots of good young players but they didn't have many stars. This could be a great story to write for the newspaper. 'What's his name?' he asked with pen and notepad ready.

'Zlatan Ibrahimović.'

Rune was looking forward to the training session

the next day. The first thing he noticed about Zlatan was his height. 'Very tall – six foot four?' Rune wrote down in his notepad. His next note was 'Wow'. Rune had expected Zlatan to be a classic big striker – great in the air but a bit clumsy with the ball at his feet. But there was nothing clumsy about Zlatan's feet. The journalist had never seen such skill.

'How is that possible?' Rune said to himself as Zlatan controlled a high ball perfectly and dribbled past three defenders with ease. The older players tried to foul him but Zlatan was too strong and too good at shielding the ball. Rune laughed at the scene. Suddenly, the striker used his quick feet to escape and his shot flew past the goalkeeper.

'You were right,' Rune told Hasse when the practice was over. 'That kid *is* magical – he's like The Hulk!'

'He's still got a lot to learn about the professional game but there's plenty of talent there.'

'The senior defenders didn't look happy at all – he made them look like fools.'

'Zlatan's never been worried about upsetting people!' Hasse laughed.

Rune was desperate to get an interview with this youngster. He had a feeling that it might be very interesting. He found him in the car park.

'Hi Zlatan, how's it going?'

'Good, thanks,' he replied. Everyone at Malmö knew who Rune Smith was and everyone liked him. 'Did you like what you saw today?'

'I loved it! How do you feel about answering a few questions for the readers?'

'Sure,' Zlatan said. He had never been shy. All of the best players did media interviews and now was a good chance to tell his story and spread the word about his talent. He was nineteen years old and he wanted to be famous.

'So, Malmö have been relegated to the second division,' Rune said as they sat drinking coffee. 'The club is in crisis – are you the future?'

Zlatan laughed. 'Of course I am! With me up front, we'll win the league and get back to the top.'

'Is that a promise?' Rune asked with a smile. He had never seen such confidence in a young Swedish player. It was a breath of fresh air.

Zlatan nodded. 'And in three years, I'll be playing for Inter Milan like Ronaldo.'

Rune was very pleased with the interview. He knew that it would be very popular. 'Remember the name: ZLATAN' was the headline that he chose, and when the newspaper published the article, Sweden went crazy. Zlatan was suddenly one of the most popular footballers in the country. More and more people came to watch him play and more fans wanted photos and autographs.

Zlatan! Zlatan! Zlatan!

The naughty kid from Rosengård was becoming a superstar, and he loved the attention. He was talking the talk brilliantly but how good was he at walking the walk? He was focused on entertaining the fans with his tricks and scoring lots of goals. There was even talk about foreign clubs wanting to sign him.

'Zlatan, we want you to sign a professional contract,' Hasse told him.

'Why? Are other teams trying to buy me?' he asked, but the sporting director ignored his question.

'This is a great opportunity for you to develop. One full season in the second division will be a great experience for you. You can take us back to the top.'

Zlatan liked the sound of that, especially when they offered him more money. He knew he still had a lot to learn and he felt comfortable at Malmö. He signed the new contract and bought a brand new car to celebrate.

His friends in Rosengård were very proud. 'Zlatan, you're the best!' they said as they drove through the streets, playing loud music.

On the pitch, though, he was still having problems. The fans loved the skills but his teammates weren't very impressed by his goalscoring record.

'He's meant to be a striker, not a circus act!'

'He thinks he's the best player in the world – someone needs to tell him that he's not!'

'Half of the time, he just walks around offside. Does he even know the rules?'

Zlatan never listened to the criticisms but he knew that he needed to be more consistent. There were some magical moments, but also whole games where Zlatan was very quiet. Because of the media attention, defenders knew who he was and they didn't give Zlatan any space. They kicked him and insulted him all match long.

'It's not my fault that the newspapers are saying

that I'm Sweden's best young player,' Zlatan complained to his strike partner, Niclas Kindvall. 'Sometimes I make mistakes – I'm still young!'

'I know, there's way too much pressure on you,' Niclas agreed. 'Just focus on scoring more goals – that's the only way to prove you're worth it.'

Zlatan finished the season as the team's top scorer but twelve goals in the second division wasn't enough. At least Malmö would be back in the first division the following season and Zlatan couldn't wait to challenge himself against better opponents.

Even so, the club was in a lot of debt and Hasse knew that a good transfer fee for Zlatan could save Malmö. Lots of scouts watched him play every week and soon clubs would start to make offers.

'Would you like to go on a tour of Europe?' Hasse asked him during the summer break. 'We'll go to England, France and Italy.'

Zlatan had never left Sweden before. 'Sure!' he said. He had a feeling that exciting times were just around the corner.

CHAPTER 11

LEAVING SWEDEN

'Would you like to come and have a trial at Arsenal?'
Arsène Wenger asked when they met at the club's
training ground. For the first time ever, Zlatan fell
silent. Out of the window of Wenger's office, he
could see Dennis Bergkamp and Thierry Henry
warming up on the perfect green pitches. It was one
of the coolest places that Zlatan had ever seen.

He was always ready to prove himself, especially
against legends like Bergkamp and Henry, but Hasse
said no.

'Zlatan is one of the best young players in Europe
– you should know enough about him already!'

They visited Monaco and Verona too but Hasse
couldn't agree a deal for his star. Zlatan had a great

time travelling around Europe but he wanted to know where he would be playing next season.

'Don't worry, we'll get things sorted very soon,' Hasse reassured him when they arrived back in Sweden.

Out of all the scouts chasing Zlatan, one stood out. John Steen Olsen, from Denmark, worked for the famous Dutch club Ajax. Ajax had an amazing youth academy, so John was only seeking the very best talents. But after the first time he watched Zlatan in 2000, he kept coming back.

John rarely attended Swedish second division matches but 'Zlatan-mania' was just starting so he wanted to see how good this arrogant young kid really was. Ajax played a nice, passing game and a big target man wouldn't fit their style. But John saw straightaway that Zlatan had fantastic technique for his height. He didn't want to head the ball in the air; he wanted the ball at his feet, where he could dribble past defenders.

'He's something special,' John said to himself.

Zlatan didn't always make the best decisions but John could tell that he understood the game and was always thinking about what he would do next. With some really good Ajax coaching, he could be amazing.

'I've got a kid at Malmö called Ibrahimović,' John informed Leo Beenhakker, the Ajax technical director. 'I think he might be the real deal but I want to watch him play a few more games.'

John spoke to Zlatan and they became friends. Underneath the cocky public image, he was a good kid who was serious about working hard to become the best. With each game he saw, John noticed more and more club scouts in the crowd. When he heard about Zlatan's trip to Arsenal, he called Leo again. 'The interest is growing – if we want this guy, we need to act now!'

John and Leo went together to watch Zlatan play in a friendly in Spain. Even the warm-up impressed Leo. 'You can see that he has that winning attitude. He stands tall with a confident face that says losing isn't even an option!'

Just half an hour later, Leo was ready to make Malmö an offer. The team were on the attack and Zlatan got the ball just outside the penalty area.

There were a lot of defenders around, so he had to think fast and do something unexpected. No-one could do the unexpected like Zlatan. He lobbed it over the first defender and ran into the box. The ball bounced up at the perfect angle for a backheel, so Zlatan flicked it cleverly over the second defender. It was like he was back on the Rosengård estate playing street football. As the ball came down, he volleyed it with his left foot past the goalkeeper and into the net. He ran across the pitch to celebrate his goal, with a scream of 'It's show time!'

'Wow!' Leo shouted. He knew that they weren't the only ones that had just seen that moment of magic. They needed to act fast.

'He's a born entertainer,' John laughed. 'Zlatan knows we're here and he did that to impress us.'

'We want that kid,' Leo told Hasse as soon as he found him after the match. 'Can we meet him?'

'We're a little busy,' replied Hasse, who was determined to get a good deal for Zlatan.

'Bring him to our hotel in an hour,' Leo said.

Zlatan felt nervous as he went to meet Leo. Hopefully, John had told him about his character.

Zlatan wanted to make a good impression but he couldn't pretend to be someone else. If they wanted him, they would have to know what he was like.

'At Ajax, our kids listen to what the coaches say,' Leo told him and Zlatan was impressed by his no-nonsense style. 'If you don't want to learn, we'll kick you out.'

Zlatan nodded and waited for an offer. A few weeks later, the deal was done.

'Congratulations!' Hasse was thrilled. 'You'll earn four times more and they'll buy you a car too.'

'Great but I want to choose my car!' Zlatan said as he signed the contract.

The only thing left to settle was the transfer fee. John Carew had just become Scandinavia's most expensive player when he signed for Valencia for £5 million. Zlatan really wanted to beat that.

When Hasse and Leo had finished their meeting, he asked, 'So how much did they pay for me?'

'£6 million,' Hasse whispered. The news wouldn't be reported until later in the day.

Zlatan was shocked. 'What did you say?'

'£6 million.'

At nineteen, Zlatan was already Sweden's most expensive footballer. He couldn't believe it; things had moved so fast. To think that a few years ago, he had nearly given up on football.

When the newspapers wrote about the transfer, his phone didn't stop ringing.

'Congratulations, King Zlatan!'

'Good luck, mate!'

He was all over Swedish TV too and his mother Jurka phoned him in a panic.

'Son, what have you done now?' she asked. 'I just saw your face on Channel 1.'

Zlatan laughed. 'Don't worry, mum, it's good news – I've just signed for Ajax in Holland!'

He travelled to Amsterdam for the press conference. With all of the cameras watching, he tried to look as stylish as possible in a pink jumper and a brown leather jacket. He had a big smile on his face as he held up the red-and-white shirt with Number 9 on the back.

'I'm ready to become the best!' he told the Dutch media.

The Malmö fans would always love him but other

Swedish fans still hated Zlatan. They thought he was too arrogant and overrated. Before he left Sweden, Zlatan wanted to prove them wrong. In an away game at Djurgården, the fans booed him persistently. Malmö were winning 2–0 but their big defenders had kept Zlatan quiet by fouling him.

'You're rubbish, you can't even score!' the fans were shouting.

Zlatan got the ball just inside the Djurgården half and ran at the defenders just like Ronaldo had taught him. One dived in for a tackle and Zlatan dribbled past him easily. Three of them tried to stop him but Zlatan was in the mood to score. From the edge of the penalty area, he struck the ball into the bottom corner.

Goooooooooooooooooooaaaaaaaaaaaaaaaaaaaaaaaaa aaaaaaalllllllllllllllllllll!!!!!!

When the final whistle went, Zlatan expected the Djurgården fans to be angry with him but instead they joined the Malmö fans to ask for his autograph.

Zlatan, Zlatan, Super Zlatan!

He had conquered Sweden and now it was time for his next big challenge.

CHAPTER 12

FIRST IMPRESSIONS AT AJAX

'Welcome to Ajax,' the coaches said, shaking Zlatan's hand. He could tell that they were going to be very strict. Sportpark De Toekomst, his new club's training complex, was so much better than anything he had ever seen before in Sweden. There were running tracks, basketball courts and lots of beautiful green football pitches. The biggest one even had stands for spectators. 'This is why they're so good at developing players,' Zlatan thought to himself.

It was a lovely, sunny day and the last thing he wanted to do was lots of hard sprinting. But that's what he had to do. He could tell that his teammates were very fit and very quick. He thought back to Malmö when he used to take the bus instead of running 'The Mile'. There was no way that he would get away with that at Ajax.

'Faster, Zlatan!' the coaches shouted. 'You're not on your summer holiday anymore!'

Zlatan was exhausted and sweat was dripping down his face. He was their big new signing and he had to prove himself. He pushed his arms and legs harder.

'That's better!' the coaches said. The manager, Co Adriaanse, had told them to be as tough as possible with him.

Zlatan felt more comfortable in the passing drills. He knew he had good technique, especially in small spaces. The coaches seemed happy as they walked around the different groups. All of the players had brilliant close control, even the defenders. Zlatan wasn't a big fish in a small pond anymore.

He had heard all about the rules at Ajax – all of their teams played a certain type of passing, flowing football. The problem was that Zlatan loved to break rules.

'We're going to play a game of two-touch football,' the coach told them, handing orange bibs to half of the players. Zlatan hated wearing bibs but he stayed quiet. As a striker he discovered he would be playing against another Scandinavian – defender André Bergdølmo.

'So it's Sweden vs Norway,' Zlatan joked. He loved to create rivalries, even in training.

André said nothing and walked away. 'Who is this cocky kid?' he wondered.

After five minutes, Zlatan had only got the ball once. As the Number 9 he was meant to wait up front for the ball to arrive but he became bored. He didn't care about numbers. He ran back into defence, took one touch to control the ball and then another to shift it towards the right.

'Hey, that's two touches already!' one of the players shouted.

'Shut up – there's no referee!' Zlatan replied angrily. In a real game, you could take as many touches as you liked. So why were they practising this?

'You better go and score now,' his teammates warned him.

Zlatan was desperate to make a big first

impression. He dribbled past one player, then another and another and another. His teammates stopped to watch in amazement. It looked like he was dancing and the ball was glued to his boot. No-one could stop him as he ran through and scored.

'Is that good enough?' he said as he walked back to the halfway line. They would all respect him now.

André had never seen a striker like Zlatan. He had everything – height, strength, close control and incredible skill. Trying to mark him in training was an absolute nightmare, but André tried his best to put him off.

'For a big guy, you don't like heading the ball, do you?' he said, giving Zlatan a little shove in the back.

It seemed to be Zlatan's only weakness. But he was used to these kinds of comments. 'Why would I use my head when my feet are this good?' he replied, giving a little shove back.

After a while, Adriaanse came up to André. He looked really angry.

'What's going on? You haven't tackled him once!'

'There's nothing I can do,' was André's defence. He didn't like being embarrassed in front of his teammates. 'This is only training. You don't want me to injure him, do you?'

Adriaanse shook his head and walked away. He could tell that his new striker was going to cause lots of problems in the season ahead. He just hoped that there would be many more goals than red cards.

'I guess Sweden won today,' Zlatan said at the end of the session. He was pleased with his first impression.

'Let's see what you can do in a real match,' André replied as he stormed off to the showers.

CHAPTER 13

NEW CLUB, NEW COUNTRY

'John, come and have a ride in my new car!' Zlatan called when he saw the Ajax scout at the training complex. His brand new Mercedes convertible was shining in the sun. In his flat, he had a king-size bed, a huge TV and a Playstation. Zlatan felt like the coolest guy in Europe.

When he arrived alone in Amsterdam, the club introduced him to one of his new teammates.

'Hi, I'm Maxwell,' he said shaking hands. 'I'm from Brazil.'

'Cool, do you know Ronaldo?' Zlatan asked him.

Maxwell laughed, 'Why is that everyone's first question?'

They became good friends and Zlatan often stayed at his flat instead of his own. Zlatan had a nice car and a nice TV but he didn't have any money. Just like when he used to live with his dad, there was nothing in the fridge and he was really hungry.

'Come round and I'll cook you dinner,' Maxwell told him. He was a really kind person and he helped Zlatan adapt to his new surroundings.

Ajax was a very big club. Five years earlier, they had won the Champions League with world class players like Patrick Kluivert, Edgar Davids and Clarence Seedorf. For a young player, there was nowhere better to develop your skills. But the club hadn't won the Dutch league in three years and that was a major problem. So expectations were very high for their new record signing.

'You scored some good goals today, Zlatan,' Co Adriaanse, the Ajax manager said after training one day, 'but you played some poor passes too. You need to do better.'

Playing against some of Europe's best teams was a new experience for Zlatan. At Malmö, he always had lots of time on the ball to show off his skills. But the top defenders in Holland didn't give him any time at all. The football was so much faster.

'Come on, Zlatan!' Adriaanse shouted. 'You've got to be quicker there!'

The fans loved it when he performed great tricks and dribbled past players but they became angry when he looked like he wasn't trying hard enough.

'You're offside, Zlatan – move!'

'We don't pay you to stand still!'

Above all, Zlatan needed to score more goals. As Ajax's central striker there was a lot of pressure on him to find the net in every match. After a few poor games, he was demoted to the bench. He was young and far from home; at times, it was very difficult for him.

'I'm trying really hard,' he told Leo. 'I don't know what more I can do.'

'Don't worry,' the Ajax technical director replied. 'Be patient and everything will be fine.'

Further good advice came from Marco Van Basten, the youth team coach, and a legend of football. Zlatan had taken Van Basten's famous Number 9 shirt at Ajax, and really respected him, so listened carefully to every word he said.

'Football is a team sport and you have to trust your teammates,' said Van Basten. 'You can't do it on your own. If you pass the ball, the team will try their best to get it back to you. Believe in them and you will get better.'

Zlatan wasn't playing street football anymore – he needed to work together with the other players in order to win. It was a difficult learning curve for him. He wasn't sleeping well and he wasn't eating healthy food. When not training or playing, he spent hours and hours in front of the Playstation in his flat. He wasn't enjoying his football at all, and he missed Sweden and his family and friends.

'I'm not the same player that I was at Malmö,' he told his dad when he went home for the weekend.

'No, you're not the Old Zlatan right now,' Šefik said, 'but you'll get there. I think you're trying too hard to impress. Go back to the way you used to play in Rosengård.'

Further support wasn't far away. One day in

Malmö, he watched a beautiful blonde woman getting out of a taxi. She looked cool and successful in her smart business suit and high heels, and she had a confident attitude that Zlatan loved. When he saw her driving around in a brand new black Mercedes, he knew this was his perfect woman. Zlatan found out who she was from a friend and sent her a text message.

'Hi, how's it going? I've seen you around. I drive the red Ferrari.'

The woman's name was Helena. They went for lunch a few times and they got on really well. Zlatan had never met anyone like her. She had worked hard to get a really good job and she didn't care that he was a superstar footballer. She wasn't interested in being a celebrity.

'Zlatan, you're a crazy guy and you wear terrible clothes but you're a lot of fun,' she told him and it was the best thing he'd ever heard.

With Helena in his life, he felt like he could do anything. He settled down and didn't do as many stupid things with his friends anymore. Off the football pitch, he was a new Zlatan but on it, he was determined to revive the old Zlatan. He returned to Holland, with the old fire back in his belly.

Ajax had a new manager, Ronald Koeman, who wanted to get the best out of Zlatan. He knew that he was the club's best striker and so he pushed him hard to prove it. Zlatan never gave up – he always believed in himself. In the final of the Holland Cup, in May 2002, Ajax were losing 2–1 to Utrecht. With fifteen minutes to go, Koeman called on Zlatan.

'Go and show what you can do.'

The atmosphere in the stadium was incredible. It was show time. Zlatan couldn't wait to get out there and make a difference. He hit the crossbar with a shot but it looked like Ajax were facing defeat. Then in injury time, Wamberto scored an equaliser. The crowd went wild.

'It's golden goal in extra time,' Koeman told his players. 'We're on top now and we need to score quickly.'

Five minutes later, the ball came to Zlatan in the box. There were three defenders around him but he was the tallest and the strongest, and he was determined to score. Zlatan chested it down and smashed the ball into the bottom corner.

Gooooooooooooooooooooooooaaaaaaaaaaaaaaaaaaa aaaaaaaaaaallllllllllllllllllll!!!

Zlatan ripped his shirt off and ran across the pitch with his teammates chasing him. It was a brilliant moment to end a difficult first season. This was why he played football – to be the match-winner in the biggest matches.

'Zlatan! Zlatan! Zlatan!' the Ajax fans chanted as they waved their red-and-white scarves above their heads.

As they celebrated on the pitch afterwards, Koeman put an arm around Zlatan. 'Thank you!' he shouted in his ear.

Zlatan couldn't wait to lift his first club trophy. He kissed the cup and raised it high into the air.

'You really deserved that today,' Maxwell said to him as they danced and sang 'We are the Champions'.

Ajax won the Dutch league too that season but Zlatan still wasn't satisfied. Six goals in twenty-four games wasn't a good record for a striker. It was time to step up and become the club's star player. But first, Zlatan was off to the World Cup in Japan and South Korea.

CHAPTER 14

GROWING UP

Zlatan was very excited about playing in a World Cup. He'd watched Romário and Bebeto on TV in 1994 and then Rivaldo and Ronaldo at the 1998 tournament. There was no bigger stage for football. He had been worried that Sweden wouldn't select him but in the end, they did.

Zlatan loved playing for his country. He could have played for Bosnia or Croatia instead because of his parents, but he felt Swedish. He was a child of Rosengård, and had grown up and learnt his football skills there. He had played seven games for the Swedish Under-21s when he was called up to the senior squad for the first time. Everyone had heard so much about Zlatan and it was now time to see if he was good enough at international level.

He was very proud to be picked. It was an honour
to train alongside players like Henrik Larsson and
Patrik Andersson, both of whom had helped Sweden
finish third at the 1994 World Cup. Henrik had also
won the Golden Boot award that year for scoring the
most goals in European leagues. Zlatan tried to stay
quiet and fit in but he was always the player that the
media wanted to talk to.

'Who are your heroes on the pitch?' one journalist
asked him.

'Henrik Larsson and Ronaldo are amazing and I
try to learn from them,' Zlatan began and then he
remembered his public image. 'But there's only one
Zlatan!'

He had made his national debut for Sweden in
January 2001. It was a Nordic Championship friendly
against the Faroe Islands and he really hoped to at
least play a few minutes. It was heading towards a
boring 0–0 draw, the perfect time for Zlatan to come
on and entertain. The match still ended goalless
but at least he was now an international footballer.
It was a really cool feeling but scoring his first goal
for Sweden several months later, in a World Cup

qualifier against Azerbaijan, was even better. The fans chanted his name loudest of all.

At the 2002 World Cup, Marcus Allbäck and Henrik Larsson would be Sweden's first-choice strikers but Zlatan hoped he would get a chance.

'At some point, we'll need something special and then it will be show time,' he told defender Olof Mellberg at the training camp.

Zlatan loved the atmosphere in Japan and South Korea. It was great to be part of such a huge, global tournament. This was what football was all about. Sweden were in the 'group of death' with England, Argentina and Nigeria. They would have to play really well to make it through to the second round. Zlatan didn't play at all in their first two matches. The coaches preferred the older, more experienced players but the fans were calling for their young superstar.

Zlatan! Zlatan! Zlatan!

In the final group game against Argentina, he replaced Henrik with a few minutes to go. It was nice to get onto the pitch but Zlatan needed more time. In the second round, Sweden faced the surprise team of the tournament, Senegal. Henrik scored early on but it was 1–1 with ten minutes to go. When he came on, Zlatan ran and ran but he couldn't score. In extra time, Senegal scored and Sweden were knocked out.

'In four years' time, I'll be our number-one striker and we'll do better!' the undeterred Zlatan told his dad when he returned home.

Back at Ajax that autumn, Zlatan faced a new challenge – the Champions League. Against Lyon, he got the ball on the left side of the penalty area. He used his skill to skip between two defenders and then he shot into the far corner of the net.

'Two goals in your Champions League debut,' his new strike partner, Jari Litmanen said with a smile. 'I think you're going to enjoy this tournament!'

But things weren't going so well for Zlatan in the Dutch league. He wasn't scoring enough goals for Ajax and the coaches were criticising him for not helping his team in defence.

'That's not my job!' Zlatan complained to Van Basten. They talked every week and Zlatan was very grateful for his support.

'Don't listen to them,' Van Basten said. 'Your job is to attack – if you waste energy chasing back, you won't have enough energy to score goals.'

Zlatan also asked him about playing in Italy. Van Basten had won lots of trophies for AC Milan and there were rumours that Roma wanted to sign Zlatan.

'You're not ready for that yet,' Van Basten told him. 'You need to be a better goalscorer first because you don't get many chances in Serie A. It's a tough league for a young striker.'

Zlatan agreed to wait but he wanted a new agent who understood him better. Maxwell said he had the perfect man – Mino Raiola.

'He's a tough guy,' Maxwell warned but Zlatan liked the sound of him.

When they met up, Zlatan expected Mino to talk about how he was one of the best young players in the world and lots of big clubs wanted to buy him.

Instead, Mino said of Zlatan's goalscoring record, 'Your stats are rubbish.'

'What?' Zlatan was shocked.

'You think you're really great, don't you?' Mino continued. 'You've got fast cars and fancy watches but you can't score goals. You've won two Dutch league titles but this season you only scored fifteen in thirty-one games.'

'That's not fair!'

'You're lazy, Zlatan,' Mino said, looking him straight in the eyes. 'That's your problem. If you work with me, will you do what I say?'

'Okay,' he agreed. He liked the way the agent wasn't trying to impress him.

'Right, well the first thing you need to do is sell the cars and the watches. The second thing you need to do is work a lot harder in training.'

Zlatan nodded. He felt like a naughty schoolboy again but Mino was right. When people told him he was great, he believed them. But it was time to really walk the walk if he wanted to play for one of the best teams in the world.

CHAPTER 15

ITALY

At Euro 2004 in Portugal, Sweden were flying. After winning 5–0 against Bulgaria, their next opponents were Italy, tipped to win the tournament because of first-rate players like Gianluigi Buffon, Fabio Cannavaro and Christian Vieri. But Zlatan was really determined to beat them. He wanted to impress the whole world, and one person in particular: his dad Šefik, watching in the crowd.

'I'm going to score for you!' he told his dad before kick-off.

With five minutes left against Italy, Sweden were losing 1–0. Zlatan had played well but the opposition's defence was brilliant. The corner came in from the left and it was flicked into the six-yard box. There were lots of players around but Zlatan beat Buffon to the ball. It bounced too low for a header but too high for a normal shot. Luckily, Zlatan had lots of cool tricks. He leaped into the air and backheeled the ball towards the top corner. Vieri was standing on the post but he couldn't stop the goal.

Zlatan watched the ball land in the net and then raised his arms into the air. It was an amazing goal and a really important one too. He ran towards the Sweden fans, who were going wild in the stands. Henrik, Marcus and the rest of the team chased after him and jumped on him.

'What a goal!' Henrik shouted.

Sweden's Euro 2004 was over in the quarter-finals when they lost on penalties to Holland, but Zlatan's reputation was bigger than ever, especially in Italy.

'I have some news,' Mino told him when he got back to Amsterdam. 'I think Juventus are going to make an offer for you.'

Zlatan couldn't believe it. They were one of the biggest clubs in Europe and they had won the Italian league twice in three years. They had Buffon, Pavel Nedvěd and Alessandro Del Piero.

'Wow! When can we talk to them?' he asked.

'Be patient,' Mino said. 'I'm doing my best.'

With Juventus watching him, Zlatan worked harder than ever. Against Breda, he received the ball with his back to goal. He ran past one defender to create some space and then pretended to shoot. As the defender went to block, Zlatan moved the ball to the left. There were four players between him and the goal but he danced his way between them, moving the ball from one foot to the other and then back. When he shot into the bottom corner, Zlatan raised his arms in the air. It was the best goal he had ever scored.

'That was like Maradona!' Jari shouted as they celebrated. It was voted the Best Goal of the Year in Holland.

Zlatan was ready to move on but his transfer to Juventus wasn't yet completed. Ajax didn't want to sell him and the Italian club was having doubts too. Eventually, though, Mino persuaded both sides to sign the deal.

'Dad, I've signed for Juventus!' Zlatan said happily. Helena was coming to Italy with him and he couldn't wait to start their new life there.

'Congratulations, son,' Šefik replied. 'I'm very proud of you!'

In Turin, Zlatan was presented to the Juventus fans. They cheered his name but many had doubts about him being a top goalscorer. Manager Fabio Capello wanted Zlatan to work hard on his shooting and he asked his assistant, Italo Galbiati, to help.

After a long training session, Zlatan was about to head off to the showers but Italo threw a ball to him. 'Shoot!' One of the youth keepers was waiting in goal. Zlatan hit it powerfully into the top corner and Italo quickly threw him another ball in a slightly different position.

'Keep going!' he shouted.

Half an hour later, Zlatan had taken nearly a hundred shots and he was exhausted. He sat on the grass and looked at all of the balls scattered around the goal.

'Well done,' Italo said, patting him on the back.

'We'll do that again tomorrow, with Buffon as keeper!'

Zlatan was getting better and better with Capello's support. He was careful about his diet and he went to the gym to add extra muscle. It was hard, boring work but it would be worth it on the pitch.

'Those dirty Italian defenders won't be able to cope with me!' he told his manager. He felt quicker and more powerful around the penalty area.

'That's good because it's very difficult for strikers in Italy,' Capello told him. 'Serie A has the best defences in the world – the fans believe stopping goals is just as important as scoring them.'

In his Serie A debut against Brescia, Zlatan got the ball with his back to goal. He turned and ran but it looked like there was nowhere to go. Suddenly, with strength and skill, he cut inside past two defenders and shot at goal. It was a simple save for the goalkeeper but he made a mistake and the ball trickled over the line. It wasn't one of Zlatan's best strikes but he was off the mark in Italy.

'They all count!' he joked with Fabio Cannavaro as they celebrated.

Zlatan was keeping club legend Alessandro Del Piero on the bench and the fans voted him Player of the Month for December 2004. He wasn't quite the complete striker yet, however. In the three months from January 2005, Zlatan only scored one goal.

'You played really badly today,' Capello shouted at him in the dressing room one day and Zlatan knew he was right. Scoring goals was all about confidence and at that moment, he didn't have any at all. He needed to find the 'Old Zlatan' again. Capello showed him videos of Van Basten to help him.

'Watch the way he moves around the box,' he said. 'You need to be clever like that.'

Zlatan decided to get really serious about scoring goals. That was his main job in the team. If he displayed his great skills but Juventus lost, the fans booed him. But even if he scored an ugly goal, they cheered his name. His recovery began with two goals against Fiorentina in April 2005 but there was more to come later that month.

As he waited for kick-off against Lecce, Zlatan looked really focused. He was picturing some of the movements that he would make in order to score goals.

Juventus were on the attack and Zlatan was in lots of space on the left. He called for the ball and Mauro Camoranesi played a great pass. He had Alessandro to his right but Zlatan was only thinking about shooting. A defender tried to tackle him but he dribbled past him and put the ball through the goalkeeper's legs.

'Great goal!' Alessandro shouted. 'I thought you'd try to do a few more skills before you scored.'

He smiled. 'No, this is the new Zlatan!'

Pavel ran at the centre of the Lecce defence and Zlatan ran down the left. When the pass came, he didn't even take a touch to control the ball. He shot straight away and it thundered into the bottom corner.

The fans went wild and on the touchline, Capello nodded and gave a rare smile. Zlatan was becoming a real goalscorer.

In the second-half, Pavel played the ball to him again. Zlatan was outside the penalty area, with one defender in front of him. The 'Old Zlatan' would have tried to dribble but the 'New Zlatan' took one touch and curled the ball into the net.

'You made that look so easy!' Pavel said as they celebrated the hat-trick.

Zlatan shrugged. Scoring lots of goals was pretty cool.

CHAPTER 16

JUVENTUS TO INTER

'That was a pretty good first season in Italy,' Mino told Zlatan during the summer break. Zlatan had been Juventus's top scorer with sixteen goals as they won the league title. Even at the age of twenty-three, he already had a lot of winner's medals and, apart from a couple of silly angry outbursts, he was growing up to become a world-class striker. 'So what's the next target?'

'Twenty league goals,' Zlatan replied without thinking.

'Okay, but you know Trezeguet is back?' Mino reminded him.

David Trezeguet was the club's number-one striker but he had been injured for a lot of the previous season. Zlatan would have to fight really hard to keep his place.

'I'm not moving for anyone!' he told Mino.

Against Roma, the ball was kicked down the pitch from defence. Zlatan was on the halfway line and he cleverly flicked the ball behind him and ran. The defender tried to stop him but Zlatan was faster and stronger. He dribbled towards goal and as he entered the penalty area, he hit the ball with the outside of his right foot into the top corner.

Goooooooooooooooooooooooaaaaaaaaaaaaaaaaaaaaa aaaaaallllllllllllllllll!!!!!!!!!!

That was one he would have been proud to score on the Rosengård estate. As the Juventus fans went crazy in the stands, Zlatan blew kisses to them. He loved to entertain them and make them happy.

Juventus were top of the league but something strange was going on. Zlatan was ready to sign a new contract but the club kept delaying.

'This doesn't feel right,' Mino said when he tried to call the managing director for the twentieth time. 'Something is wrong.'

When Zlatan wasn't happy, he didn't play as well

as he normally did. He felt heavy and clumsy and he wasn't scoring enough goals. Alessandro and David were a good partnership in attack and Capello put Zlatan on the bench.

'Mino, I think it's time for me to leave Juventus,' he said.

Slowly, it became clear that Juventus were involved in a big corruption scandal. When the season was over, the club was relegated to Serie B and lost its league titles. Zlatan didn't know what to do.

'I love this club and the fans but I can't stay here and play in the second division,' he told his dad. 'I'm twenty-four – these should be the best years of my football career!'

'Son, you need to do what's best for you,' Šefik said and so Zlatan called Mino. 'Please get me out of here as quickly as possible.'

In the meantime, he was off to Germany for the 2006 World Cup. Sweden nearly didn't qualify for the tournament but Zlatan saved the day. In the last minute of the playoff against Hungary, he got the ball in the penalty area. There were lots of defenders around him. Zlatan moved the ball to the right but the defenders weren't worried – he was too wide to shoot, they thought. But Zlatan smashed the ball into the top corner from an impossible angle.

Zlatan! Zlatan! Zlatan!

He was the national hero again and he loved it. Expectations were high for the tournament but Zlatan had a groin injury. He carried on playing but he couldn't really help his country.

'I can't concentrate,' he told Mino after their defeat to Germany put Sweden out of the World Cup. 'I need to find a new club.'

'Okay, who would you prefer to play for – AC Milan or Inter Milan?' his agent asked.

That was a very difficult question. AC Milan were the more successful team with players like Paolo Maldini and Andriy Shevchenko, but one of Zlatan's heroes Ronaldo had played for Inter. Playing for them would be a bigger challenge and that's what Zlatan wanted.

The Zlatan deal was signed in August 2006, just after Inter had won Serie A for the first time in seventeen years. 'This is our biggest signing since

Ronaldo in 1997,' the excited Inter Milan president told the media. Zlatan was very happy to hear that. £20 million was a big transfer fee to live up to but he could handle the pressure.

'I'm here to make a difference and win the league!' he told the media. The fans loved that.

There was, though, one other very important reason for joining Inter – Maxwell.

'Are you following me?' his Brazilian friend asked with a big smile on his face as Zlatan arrived at training. 'Just let me know whenever your fridge is empty!'

It was nice to see a friendly face and Zlatan knew that he was going to be happy here. He was very impressed by his other new teammates. Javier Zanetti, Patrick Vieira, Luís Figo and Hernán Crespo were all top players with lots of experience.

'If we work really hard together, we can beat AC Milan and Roma!' Zlatan told them in training. He vowed to lead Inter to victory. He had never been so determined to win.

There were many different nationalities represented at Inter but Zlatan talked to everyone

and the players became one big family. As he had
learnt at Juventus, teamwork was key.

In the first league match of the season against
Fiorentina, Zlatan set up the first goal for Esteban
Cambiasso. In the second half, Esteban returned the
favour. He played a great pass over the defence and
Zlatan was through on goal. He calmly waited for the
ball to bounce and then shot past the goalkeeper.

Zlatan ran to his teammates to celebrate. 'This is
our season!' he shouted.

Zlatan was very happy. He was playing well for a
great team and he now had a son to think about too.
He and Helena decided to call the boy Maximilian,
a strong name for a small boy. His birth was the
proudest day of his life.

In the next league match, Zlatan was warming up
on the pitch and he looked up into the crowd. The
fans were holding up a big banner saying, 'Welcome
Maximilian!' It took him a little while to realise that
they were talking about his little boy. It was a lovely
moment that Zlatan would never forget.

'These supporters are the best,' he thought to
himself as he took pictures to show Helena.

In between victories, he made a very important trip back to Malmö. Zlatan had helped to build a brand new five-a-side pitch on the Rosengård estate where he had learnt all of his skills. The pitch was made of recycled old trainers like the ones they used to play in. There were bright lights all around the courtyard and so it was much safer for the local kids at night.

It was a very emotional moment to go back to Rosengård and open 'Court Zlatan'. He thought about how far he had come, both as a footballer and as a person. He was so lucky and so proud.

'I can tell you it's a lot nicer than the pitch I used to play on here!' Zlatan joked as he cut the ribbon.

On the gates of 'Court Zlatan', there was a message for the local youngsters: 'Here is my heart. Here is my history. Here is my play. Take it further.' Zlatan was the boy from the estate who had made it to the top. He really wanted to inspire others to dream big too.

As he watched the kids play their first match at 'Court Zlatan', he told them, 'There's only one Zlatan but there can be lots of great footballers from Rosengård!'

Back in Italy, Inter were unstoppable and they won the league by more than twenty points. Despite having a few injuries, Zlatan scored fifteen goals but it was all about the team performance.

'That was too easy!' Zlatan joked with Hernán as the players jumped up and down together on the pitch. There were still five games of the season left to play. In the stands, the Inter fans were having a big party. The stadium was a sea of blue-and-black flags. Zlatan took off his shirt and threw it into the crowd and then put on a new one that had 'Champions' written on the back.

'It seems like everywhere you go, you win trophies,' Hernán said.

Zlatan nodded happily. 'But I haven't won the Champions League yet!'

CHAPTER 17

PLAYING FOR 'THE SPECIAL ONE'

Zlatan's phone rang – it was 'The Special One', José Mourinho, the new Inter Milan manager. Zlatan had heard a lot about Mourinho and expected him to be very tough.

'Hello, it's José. How are you?'

'I'm good, thanks.'

'Great, well I just wanted to say that I'm looking forward to working with you next season. See you soon,' Mourinho said and then he hung up.

Zlatan was shocked by how friendly he was. Mourinho wanted to get to know his star striker and he liked that. Zlatan was one of the best players in the world now and the Serie A Player of the Year too. The new manager was relying on him.

In the dressing room, Mourinho often got angry but he also cared about his players.

'How's Vincent?' he asked. Zlatan now had a second child, a younger brother for Maxi. He loved his happy family.

'He's doing well, thanks,' Zlatan replied, 'but I don't know how my mum looked after so many kids. Helena and I are exhausted!'

Mourinho was the best manager that Zlatan had ever played for. He always knew how to get the best out of his players.

'So far today, you've all been useless,' Mourinho said at half-time when they were losing. 'Zlatan, you're not doing anything. I'll take you off if you don't work harder.'

He wanted Zlatan to score even more goals. 'You're getting better every season, so this year your target is twenty-five in the league.'

That was a lot of goals but Zlatan loved a challenge. Every time he scored, he looked over at Mourinho on the touchline but he didn't even smile.

'That's just how he is,' Mourinho's assistant told

him when he asked but Zlatan was determined to make his manager smile.

In one game, against Palermo, Zlatan got the ball a long way from goal. Normally, he would dribble past players but he was focused on scoring. He took one touch and then took a shot. The ball flew through the air, straight as a dart, and landed in the bottom corner. But Mourinho didn't smile.

He ran at the Reggina defence and dribbled past two. Zlatan saw that the goalkeeper was off his line. He chipped the ball perfectly over his head and into the top corner. But still there was no smile from the manager.

Against Fiorentina, Inter won a free-kick thirty yards from goal. Zlatan ran up and smashed it into the net. It was one of the most powerful shots ever but even then, Mourinho stayed solemn.

'What more can I do?' Zlatan asked the assistant manager.

'He wants you to be the top scorer in Italy,' he replied.

Zlatan was the joint top scorer in Italy ahead of the last game of the season against Atalanta. He needed at least one more to make Mourinho happy. After ten minutes, Zlatan was through on goal. The goalkeeper ran out to stop him but he coolly placed it in the bottom corner.

Zlatan celebrated his goal but he wanted more. With ten minutes to go, the score was 3–3. Inter Milan were already Champions of Italy but Zlatan had another award to win.

Hernán passed the ball through but there were two defenders right next to Zlatan. He fought hard and won the ball but he was facing away from goal. The years on the Rosengård estate had prepared him well for these difficult chances. Quick as a flash, he backheeled the ball past the goalkeeper and into the net.

Goooooooooooooooooooooooooooaaaaaaaaaaaaaaaaaa aaaaaaaaaaaaaaaallllllllllll!!!!!

Zlatan had done it. He took his shirt off and roared like a lion. He looked over at his manager. This time Mourinho was jumping up and down with joy.

'You did it – twenty-five!' the manager shouted, giving him a big hug. It was one of the best feelings ever.

Zlatan won the Top Goalscorer and Footballer of the Year awards. He had a lot to thank his manager for.

'If it wasn't for your grumpy face, I wouldn't have scored so many goals!' he joked.

Zlatan loved playing for such a special manager who believed in him and pushed him to keep improving his skills. But once the season was over, he started thinking about his career. Zlatan had won five Serie A titles in a row – was it time to try a different league?

'I really want to win the Champions League,' he said to his agent, Mino. 'I love it here at Inter but I'm not sure we can win it.'

'Well all of the top clubs want you,' Mino told him. 'Manchester United, Real Madrid, Barcelona...'

'Playing for Barcelona would be amazing!' Zlatan said, picturing himself alongside Lionel Messi, Xavi and Iniesta. The Spanish team had just beaten Manchester United in the Champions League final, and Maxwell was about to sign for them too.

'I'm coming with you!' Zlatan told his friend, but it wasn't a done deal yet.

When Real Madrid bought Cristiano Ronaldo and Kaká, Barcelona knew they needed to buy a new superstar of their own. Zlatan would be perfect but the problem was that Inter Milan didn't want to sell their best player.

'You can't leave!' Mourinho told him when he found out. 'We'll win the Champions League next season, I promise.'

But Zlatan had made up his mind and in the summer of 2009 Barcelona announced they were willing to pay £60 million for him. When he stepped off the airplane, there were hundreds of fans and journalists waiting for him.

'Ibra! Ibra! Ibra!'

'Welcome to Barça!'

Zlatan couldn't believe it – this really was show time. Later that evening, he walked out on to the Camp Nou pitch wearing the Barcelona shirt. There were more than 60,000 supporters in the stadium waiting just to see him do a few keepy-uppies. It was an incredible feeling to hear so many fans chanting his name.

'I wonder how loud it will be when I actually play

a match!' he said to Mino with a big smile on his face. This was massive.

Zlatan kissed the club badge on his shirt and the noise got even louder. He thought about all of the amazing footballers who had played for Barcelona – Cruyff, Maradona, Ronaldo, Messi… and now Zlatan. He had come so far from street football in Malmö. It all felt like a dream.

'I'm the happiest man in the world!' he told the media and it was true.

CHAPTER 18

BARÇA

'Wow, these guys are on a different planet!' Zlatan told his dad on the phone after his first week at Barcelona. 'I thought my technique was the best but here I'm average. Messi, Xavi and Iniesta make football look like beautiful art.'

'So you're enjoying it?' Šefik asked.

'The football is amazing but the club is like Malmö all over again,' Zlatan said. 'I'm used to being the outsider, though!'

A lot of the players had grown up together in the Barcelona youth academy, La Masia. They were very friendly but they always sat together and the manager, Pep Guardiola, seemed to give them special treatment. They were the opposite of Zlatan – these were quiet guys who didn't like fancy cars and fame. They were the best players at the best club in the best league in the world but they didn't act like it.

'Hi Zlatan, welcome to Barça!' Lionel Messi said, shaking his hand. 'It's great to have you here – the more goalscorers the better.'

Zlatan couldn't believe how down to earth they all were. They wore tracksuits instead of fashionable clothes and they drove boring cars to training. Where was their competitive, winner's attitude? They were as polite as schoolboys. Luckily, he had Maxwell and Thierry Henry to hang out with.

'I nearly joined Arsenal when I was eighteen!' he told Thierry one day. 'Wenger asked me to come on trial but Malmö wouldn't let me. Zlatan doesn't do auditions! If I'd joined Arsenal, they wouldn't have needed you.'

Thierry laughed. 'No way, you couldn't have scored as many goals as I did!'

Thierry and Zlatan were both really confident players and they got on very well. They would joke around together when the other players were being too serious. It was important that they enjoy football.

The media predicted that Zlatan would fail at
Barcelona. He was used to being his team's star
player but at Barcelona he was playing with the
number-one player in the world – Lionel Messi. This
was Messi's team. How would Zlatan cope with
being second best?

'We work hard here,' Guardiola had warned him
in pre-season. He had sold flashy players like Deco
and Ronaldinho. That wasn't the Barça way. 'There
are no superstars at this club.'

Zlatan understood; he was ready to play for the
team. They would inspire him to get better and
better. He was determined to prove everyone wrong.

In the first game of the La Liga season for 2009–
10, Barcelona were playing without Messi. The
pressure was on Zlatan to lead them to victory. With
ten minutes to go, they were winning 2–0 but he
still hadn't scored on his debut. Zlatan needed to get
a goal.

Dani Alves crossed from the right and Zlatan
waited at the back post. A defender flicked it on and
Zlatan scored with a diving header. As he lay on the
grass, his teammates jumped on him.

'Great goal!' captain Carles Puyol shouted. It felt really good to be part of such an amazing team.

Zlatan was off to a good start and he scored in each of his first five games. He was the first Barcelona player to ever do that. In the third of those games, against Atlético Madrid, it only took him two minutes to find the net. None of them were special goals but that wasn't important. With Xavi and Iniesta in midfield, he just had to convert the chances they gave him. Barcelona had signed him to score goals and that's what he was doing. The media were full of praise and he felt on top of the world. Zlatan was living his boyhood dream.

But there was only one way to really win over the Barcelona fans – score against big rivals Real Madrid. After a thigh injury, Zlatan was back just in time for *El Clásico* but he was on the bench. It was a really tense match and the atmosphere was unbelievable. The Milan derby had been brilliant but this was even better. Spain had been talking about this match for months. Who would win – Ronaldo and Kaká or Zlatan? He couldn't wait to get out on the pitch.

At half-time, Guardiola told him to get ready. 'It's

show time!' Zlatan said to himself. As he warmed up, the fans cheered his name. Zlatan clapped them back. He would have forty minutes to make the difference and make them happy.

'Go and get us a goal,' Thierry told him as he came off but Zlatan didn't need telling.

Dani Alves got the ball on the right and ran forward. Zlatan made a run into the penalty area, cleverly placing himself between the Madrid centre-backs. Alves's cross was perfect but it was a difficult chance. Zlatan had to shoot on the volley and if he got it wrong, the fans would hate him. But if he got it right, they would love him forever. Zlatan volleyed it powerfully into the net with his left foot.

Goooooooooooooooooooooaaaaaaaaaaaaaaaaaaaaaaa aaaaaalllllllllllllllllllllll!!!!!!

It was a sensational strike in the biggest match of all. He had never heard a stadium make so much noise. With his arms outstretched, Zlatan ran towards the fans. He punched the air with joy. On the touchline, Guardiola gave a slight smile. Like Mourinho, he liked to keep challenging his striker.

'That's what we paid all that money for!'

Guardiola said to Zlatan at the final whistle. Zlatan smiled. He was the match-winner and it was the best feeling ever.

CHAPTER 19

TOUGH TIMES

After a relaxing Christmas break, Zlatan was raring to go again. He had already scored eleven goals in the 2009–10 season and he wanted to score many more.

'We're going to change our tactics,' Pep Guardiola told his Barcelona team in training. 'Instead of the 4-3-3 formation, we're going to play a 4-5-1 with Lionel playing in the centre behind Zlatan.'

Zlatan was glad that he was still in the team but he was worried about how the new system would affect his natural game.

'With Lionel playing through the middle now, I'm going to be stuck up front!' he complained to Thierry. 'I won't be free to drop deeper anymore. It's a waste – I can do more than just score goals!'

'Yes, but this team is built around Lionel,' Thierry reminded him. Thierry was usually a substitute these days.

On the pitch, Zlatan's form worsened. Barcelona were still winning all of their matches but the ball always went straight to Lionel. Lionel was scoring plenty of goals but Zlatan was struggling in his new role.

'I'm not happy,' he told his dad on the phone. In his last match, he had been sent off for kicking a defender. Things weren't going well. 'Guardiola isn't making the most of my talent. I barely touch the ball now.'

'I know it's difficult, son, but you just have to be keep working hard,' Šefik told him. 'If it's still bad at the end of the season, you can leave. But for now, you can still win the Champions League for the first time!'

That was Zlatan's number-one aim. He had left Inter Milan to join Barcelona because he was desperate to win the biggest trophy in European football. Zlatan needed to forget his problems and focus on scoring goals again.

Against Mallorca, Carles shot at goal after a corner kick, but the goalkeeper made a save. The ball bounced out and Zlatan was there to smash the ball into the net. It was another simple goal but it was the match-winner. Real Madrid were right behind Barcelona in the league and Zlatan was pleased to help his team.

'That's three in three games,' he told Maxwell. 'I'm back!'

'Your timing is perfect,' his friend said. 'We've got Arsenal in a few days!'

Zlatan couldn't wait for the Champions League quarter-final. In the tunnel before kick-off, he looked calm but there was a real focus in his eyes. He was like a hunter in the penalty area, always ready for a chance to score. Dani Alves ran down the right wing and crossed the ball to Zlatan. It was quite an easy chance but he shot high over the bar.

'How did I miss that?' Zlatan said. He couldn't believe that it was still 0–0 at half-time.

'Don't worry, you'll get lots more chances today,' Maxwell told him.

Zlatan was determined to score. In the first minute

of the second half, Gerard Piqué played a long ball forward to him. The Arsenal goalkeeper had come out of his goal to try to win the ball but Zlatan got there first and lobbed the ball over him and into the net. He was so happy to score a brilliant goal in such an important match. He ran and jumped into the arms of his teammates on the Barcelona bench. Zlatan saw that even Guardiola had a smile on his face.

Ten minutes later, Xavi passed the ball through to him. Zlatan had time to take a touch to control the ball and then his shot flew like a rocket past the goalkeeper. There was nothing he could do to stop it.

'What a great run!' Xavi said as they celebrated.

'What a great pass!' Zlatan replied. He was a team player and together Barcelona were moving towards the Champions League semi-finals.

With fifteen minutes to go, Guardiola took Zlatan off. He was very disappointed to leave the pitch when he was playing so well. By the final whistle, the score was 2–2.

'See – we need you, Zlatan!' Maxwell said.

Barcelona won the second leg and in the semifinal, they were up against Zlatan's old team, Inter Milan. He couldn't wait for the challenge.

'The last thing Mourinho said to me before I left was that Inter would win the Champions League this season,' he told Thierry. 'We can't let that happen!'

In the first leg at the San Siro, Barcelona took the lead but then Inter scored three goals. After sixty minutes, Guardiola took Zlatan off.

'I know I wasn't playing that well but he replaced me with a defender!' he moaned to Mino. Zlatan was very angry. In the big match against Mourinho, he was losing.

In the second leg, he was again substituted after sixty minutes. Inter defended really well and Zlatan didn't have any space to do something special. Barcelona crashed out of the Champions League and Zlatan felt more frustrated than ever.

'I don't understand it,' he said to Maxwell. 'When we needed to score goals, Guardiola took me off and kept Thierry on the bench. What did we do wrong? He must really hate us!'

Zlatan liked all of his teammates at Barcelona and he had tried very hard to fit in. But he felt like he was being pushed out of the club because he was different. Twenty-one goals in forty-five games was a really good record and they had won the La Liga title but that wasn't enough.

'Zlatan, I'm thinking ahead to next season,' Guardiola said when he called his striker into his office. 'We're going to change our playing style and I'm just not sure how many games you will play here.'

Zlatan wasn't shocked but he was very disappointed. It had been a dream come true to sign for Barcelona and he had given everything to help his team. But Guardiola signed David Villa, who was a goalscorer who could play on the wing. Unlike Zlatan, he was happy to play for Lionel.

'I don't want to leave,' Zlatan replied. 'I've only been here for one year and I'm determined to prove you wrong. I can play with Lionel and we can win the Champions League.'

But it was no good; his Barcelona career was over.

'You need to find me a new club,' he told Mino straight away. 'What about Real Madrid?'

'Are you joking?' Mino asked but Zlatan wanted to hurt Barcelona for letting him go. Instead, the agent made a suggestion. 'Manchester City and AC Milan are both interested.'

AC Milan had an amazing history of winning big trophies. Van Basten and Ronaldo had both played for the club.

'I'd prefer Milan,' Zlatan said. It was time to move on.

CHAPTER 20

AC MILAN

'Welcome to the best club in Milan, Zlatan!' the banners read as he arrived in Italy for the start of the 2010–11 season. He was worried that the fans might hate him because he used to play for their rivals Inter but they didn't seem to care. They were just excited about their big new signing.

Ibra! Ibra! Ibra!

Zlatan was excited too. AC Milan had big players like Clarence Seedorf, Andrea Pirlo, Alexandre Pato, Ronaldinho and Robinho in their squad but the club had signed him to be their superstar goalscorer. They hadn't won the Serie A title since 2004. What they needed was a winner.

'Wherever I go, my team wins the league!' Zlatan

joked with Ronaldinho in practice. It was nice to be in a more relaxed environment after his difficult time at Barcelona. Zlatan wasn't taking it easy, though – he was more focused than ever.

'Just pass the ball!' he shouted at Robinho on the pitch. They got on really well and Zlatan was really impressed by the Brazilian's skills. But sometimes Robinho tried to do too many tricks, just like Zlatan when he was younger.

Between them, Zlatan, Pato and Robinho were scoring lots of goals. AC Milan were at the top of the league along with their neighbours, Inter Milan. Zlatan couldn't wait for the derby match. Would the Inter fans boo him like crazy? Before the match, Zlatan shook hands with lots of his old teammates. Afterwards, they would laugh and chat but for now, they were all just thinking about winning.

The atmosphere was amazing inside the San Siro Stadium. After only four minutes of the game, Clarence played a great pass forward. Zlatan tricked Marco Materazzi and ran towards goal. As he entered the penalty area, he could tell that the defender was catching up with him, so he pretended to shoot but dragged the ball back instead. Materazzi wasn't expecting that and he kicked Zlatan's leg. Penalty!

The noise was incredible as Zlatan waited to take the spot kick. He looked calm with his hands on his hips but he was very nervous. He had to score; the AC Milan fans would be furious if he missed. When the referee blew the whistle, Zlatan ran up and hit the ball powerfully into the bottom corner. The goalkeeper dived the wrong way but he wouldn't have saved it anyway.

Goooooooooooooaaaaaaaaaaalllllllllllllllllllll!!!!!

Zlatan raised his arms above his head and Mathieu Flamini jumped up on his back. Zlatan was really happy to score but he couldn't celebrate properly; he still loved the Inter Milan fans and he had lots of respect for his old club.

The rest of the game was very tense but AC Milan held on to win 1–0. Zlatan was the hero and the fans chanted his name. It was a great feeling.

'You must be so happy!' Mino said after the game.

Zlatan smiled but his mind was already focused on the next victory. By February, he had scored thirteen goals but he was very tired.

'You need a break,' his manager, Massimiliano Allegri, told him. 'You've played every match at one hundred and ten per cent and if we're not careful you'll get injured. You're not a youngster anymore.'

Zlatan didn't want to listen. He needed to lead AC Milan to the league title. But he was pushing himself too hard. If they were to finish top of the table, they would need him to stay fit. He played fewer matches and scored fewer goals but AC Milan still won the league.

'We did it!' Clarence shouted as he hugged Zlatan.

'What did I say when I arrived here?' Zlatan replied with a big smile. 'I said I was here to win the league!'

It was a great feeling for Zlatan to have achieved his aim. It hadn't been easy for him but it was worth it to have the medal around his neck and the trophy in his hands. He walked around the pitch with his two sons: Vincent on his shoulders and Maxi by his side. Helena was there in the crowd and they waved to her. Zlatan was so happy to share this special moment with his family. The celebrations went on for hours and hours.

'I need to score more goals next season,' Zlatan decided once everything had calmed down. After a couple of weeks on holiday, he was excited to get back to playing football again. 'Fourteen isn't enough for a top goalscorer.'

Zlatan was unstoppable. Defenders knew about his quick feet but he was better than ever in the air too. Against Roma in October 2011, Alberto Aquilani crossed the ball from the right and Zlatan headed it towards goal. He was a long way from there but the ball flew past the goalkeeper.

'Your head is more powerful than my foot!' Robinho joked with him.

In the second half, Alberto crossed to him again. Zlatan didn't even move this time. His neck muscles were so powerful that the ball thundered into the net.

'I think this could be my best goalscoring year yet!' he told his dad happily that Christmas.

Šefik still watched every match that his son played and he was so proud of the way he kept improving. 'Yes, but can you beat Juventus to the title?' he asked.

Zlatan wasn't sure but he would do everything he could to lead his team to victory. Juventus didn't have a superstar like him but they had a great defence and lots of very good attackers. Zlatan scored almost every week but it wasn't quite enough to win a ninth league winner's medal in nine years.

'I'm sorry mate – we've ruined your record,' Robinho said. They were all very disappointed to lose after getting so close. 'Please don't leave!'

Zlatan didn't want to leave but AC Milan didn't have enough money to compete with Barcelona, Real Madrid and Bayern Munich. They wouldn't win the Champions League, which was what Zlatan wanted more than anything. He had scored thirty-five goals in the season, which made him the top scorer in Italy and one of the top five strikers in the world.

'I love playing in Italy but I still have some of the best years of my career ahead of me,' he told Mino at the start of summer 2012. Perhaps it was time for another big adventure.

CHAPTER 21

PROVING ENGLAND WRONG

English football fans didn't like Zlatan and he didn't really know why. One commentator had even called him 'the most overrated football player in the world'.

Ahead of Sweden's international friendly against England in late 2012, one journalist asked him, 'Why do you think that your goalscoring record against our teams is so bad?'

'What about the two goals that I scored against Arsenal?' Zlatan asked in reply. They were two of his favourite goals ever.

'Okay but you haven't scored against Manchester United, Liverpool or Tottenham in eight games.'

Zlatan smiled. 'Don't worry, I'll show you what I can do.'

Despite the many ups and downs during his Sweden career, Zlatan was back and he was now the captain of his country. As the squad had prepared for for the Euro 2012 qualifications, manager Erik Hamrén went to speak to Zlatan.

'You're our key player,' Hamrén told him. 'We have a group of very good players but they need a leader. I believe you're ready to be that leader. Please come back!'

Zlatan said yes. He was so proud to wear the captain's armband for his country. It was a sign of how far he had come as a player and as a person. He was no longer the angry young man that he had been in the past. As a thirty-year-old, he was an experienced professional who supported his teammates. As Sweden qualified for the Euro 2012 tournament in Poland and Ukraine, Zlatan scored five goals, including a hat-trick against Finland.

'We have to be fearless!' he told the team when their group was announced – England, France and Ukraine. It would be very difficult to go through to the second round. 'We're the underdogs, so let's go and surprise everyone.'

In the first match against Ukraine, Kim Källström crossed the ball and Zlatan coolly flicked it into the goal. It was a great start but Ukraine were the hosts and their supporters inspired them to a 2–1 win. Sweden would have to beat England to stay in the tournament but Zlatan couldn't do anything special as his team lost 3–2.

'We've still got one more match to play, so let's end on a high,' he told his teammates. They wanted to give a good final performance for the nation.

In the second-half, Zlatan ran forward from midfield. He was in lots of space on the edge of the penalty area if Christian Wilhelmsson could pass to him. Christian's cross from the right came to Zlatan at a difficult height. It was too low to head and so he turned his body, jumped into the air and volleyed the ball into the bottom corner. There was nothing the goalkeeper could do to save it.

'What a strike!' Kim shouted as the Sweden fans went wild. Zlatan was very pleased and it was chosen as the best goal of the whole tournament.

It was disappointing to go home so early but Zlatan had left his mark. He moved straight on to his new target – becoming Sweden's top goalscorer of all time.

'I've got thirty-five so far,' he told his teammate Kim Källström. 'Only fifteen more to go!'

In November 2012, Zlatan couldn't wait to get revenge for the defeat against England at the Euro 2012 championships. He walked out onto the pitch of Sweden's brand new stadium, and stood next to the England captain, Steven Gerrard. Zlatan had been criticised, but he loved it when people criticised him because it inspired him to be even better.

As Martin Olsson ran down the left wing, Zlatan made a great run from the back post to the front post. The cross was perfect. The defender blocked his shot but Zlatan got to the rebound first and he smashed his second shot into the top of the net. The crowd was a beautiful sea of yellow and he blew kisses to the fans. They really loved him now.

Zlatan! Zlatan! Zlatan!

England scored two quick goals to take the lead. Sweden couldn't afford to be defeated. 'Come on, we can still win this!' Zlatan shouted to his teammates. As captain, it was his job to encourage the other players. There was a good team spirit but with fifteen minutes to go, Sweden were still losing.

When Anders Svensson got the ball in midfield, he knew exactly the run that his striker was about to make. He chipped a great pass over the England defence and into Zlatan's path. With excellent technique, Zlatan chested the ball down and volleyed it past the goalkeeper, Joe Hart. On the touchline, Hamrén celebrated. He had made a great decision to bring Zlatan back into the national team. It was an incredible goal but he wasn't done yet.

With seven minutes left, he ran up to take a free-kick. It was over thirty yards away from the goal and some people expected him to cross instead of shoot. But he always believed he could score from any distance. He hit a very powerful shot that skipped over the grass. His aim was perfect; the goal went right into the bottom corner of the net. He lifted his arms with three fingers raised on each hand. He loved scoring hat-tricks.

In stoppage time, Hart came running out of his goal to clear the ball but his header didn't go very far. Zlatan watched the ball come down and got ready to do something spectacular. He loved to take risks on the football field, especially when his team was already winning. 'Show time', as Zlatan called it.

With his back to goal, he jumped into the air and kicked the ball over his head. The England defenders watched as it flew towards the goal. Zlatan was wide on the right when he shot and it was a very difficult angle to score from. Surely it wouldn't go in? One of the defenders dived to stop it but it was too late. The ball was in the net.

Goooooooaaaaaaaaaaaaaaaallllllllllllllll!!!!!!!!

Zlatan ripped off his shirt and jumped into the air. It was the kind of magical strike that he had dreamt about as a kid but now he had done it for his country against one of the best teams in the world. It was an incredible feeling. There were lots of shocked faces everywhere; they couldn't believe what Zlatan had just done.

'That's the best goal I've ever seen!' Kim shouted as they celebrated.

'Those Taekwondo classes I did as a kid were very useful!' Zlatan said.

At the final whistle, he walked coolly around the

pitch, shaking hands with the other players. Zlatan swapped shirts with Danny Welbeck and clapped the fans for all of their support. Then he went looking for the match ball; it was definitely his after scoring four goals.

'What do the England fans have to say now?' Zlatan thought to himself with a big smile on his face. It was a mistake to talk badly about him – it only made him more determined to succeed.

CHAPTER 22

THE PSG PROJECT

'Paris Saint-Germain have made a bid for you,' Mino told Zlatan on the phone as he rested after Euro 2012.

'What are AC Milan saying?' Zlatan asked. The new owners of PSG were very rich and they were spending lots of money on new players.

'It's a good offer for a thirty-year-old and they want to accept it,' his agent replied.

Zlatan would really miss Milan and the Italian fans but perhaps it was time to move on. PSG would be a really exciting project and it would be great to live in another beautiful city like Paris. Carlo Ancelotti was their manager and Zlatan had heard great things about him.

'They're about to sign Thiago Silva too,' Mino added.

'Really?' Thiago Silva was Zlatan's teammate at AC Milan and the best defender in the world. With him at the back, Blaise Matuidi and Javier Pastore in midfield and Zlatan up front, PSG could take on the world. There was one final attraction for Zlatan.

'You follow me everywhere!' Maxwell said when his friend called him to discuss the move. The Brazilian had been at PSG for six months and he was very excited to hear the news. 'You've got to sign for us – this club is the future and we need a star striker.'

It would be a big new challenge for Zlatan but he loved a challenge.

'I'm here to make history!' Zlatan told the fans who watched as he held up his PSG shirt in front of the Eiffel Tower. 'I'm going to take this team to the top.'

The crowd cheered loudly; there was a new hero in Paris. The club was delighted with their new signing. It was very difficult to find a world-class striker but now they had one. Zlatan was the big star that would help PSG become one of the best teams in Europe.

'You're now the most expensive man in football history!' Mino told him afterwards.

'What do you mean?'

'All of your transfer fees add up to £150 million.'

'Wow, that's a lot of money!' Zlatan said with a big smile on his face. He felt like he was breaking records every day.

PSG was a very different experience for Zlatan. The club had great ambition but unlike Barcelona and AC Milan, there wasn't that winning attitude. It was nearly twenty years since the club had last won the French league. Zlatan was determined to make a big difference like he had at Inter Milan.

'Come on, you can do better than that!' he shouted at his teammates on the training ground. 'We won't win things if you play bad passes like that.'

Ancelotti watched from the touchline and smiled. With Zlatan in his team, it would be impossible to lose. Maxwell had warned the other players about his friend's aggressive style but at first, they were still shocked.

'Who does he think he is – the king?'

'He can't just come here and say that we're useless!'

But they soon accepted that Zlatan was just trying to make them better players. He worked really hard and he expected everyone else to work just as hard. Everyone was learning a lot from playing with him.

'He has experience of playing for lots of big clubs, even Barcelona,' Javier told the younger players. 'Listen to him – he knows what he's talking about!'

From day one, Zlatan was a leader. Thiago Silva was injured for the first game of the season against Lorient and so Ancelotti gave Zlatan the captain's armband. He was very proud as he led his team out onto the pitch at the Parc des Princes Stadium.

But at half-time, PSG were losing 2–0. Zlatan was furious. 'That's the worst performance I've ever seen,' he shouted at the other players. 'What are we doing? It's like none of us have ever played together! We have to do something amazing in the second half.'

The ball flew through the air towards Zlatan. He was in the penalty area with two defenders around him but he was the strongest and he jumped the highest. He chested the ball down and shot into the bottom corner. 2–1.

'Come on, we can do this!' Zlatan shouted as he ran back for the kick-off.

He tried and tried to score another but he couldn't. Then in injury time, Blaise was fouled in the penalty area. It was a penalty and Zlatan had the chance to make it 2–2. There was a lot of pressure on him to score but he didn't mind. He took a short run-up and hit the ball past the goalkeeper. Zlatan raised his arms above his head. He was the hero and he made it look so easy.

After their next two games resulted in 0–0 draws, PSG desperately needed a goal against Lille. Zlatan knew it was his responsibility – this was why Ancelotti had signed him. 'Don't worry, I won't let you down today!' he told everyone in the dressing room before kick-off. He felt as confident as ever.

In the first minute, Maxwell ran down the left wing and passed inside to Jérémy Ménez. Zlatan was running into the penalty area in space and Jérémy played the ball to him. The goalkeeper came out to block the shot but Zlatan cleverly chipped the ball over him and into the net.

'I told you!' he said to his teammates as they celebrated the early goal. But ten minutes later, it was 1–1. PSG needed another goal from their superstar. Zlatan won the ball, passed to Javier and then ran forward as fast as he could. Javier's pass looked like it was too far ahead of Zlatan but he didn't give up. Just as the goalkeeper dived at his feet, Zlatan stretched out his foot and lifted the ball over him.

Goooooooooooaaaaaaaaaaallllllllllllllll!!!!!!

He ran towards the fans with his arms out like the wings of an airplane. It was a great feeling to hear all 40,000 of them chanting his name.

Zlatan! Zlatan! Zlatan!

They trusted him to win the league for the club.

CHAPTER 23

TROPHY AFTER TROPHY

'Who do you think is the best striker in the world at the moment?' a journalist asked Ronaldo.

'Ibrahimović,' the Brazilian legend replied after a pause for thought. 'He wears the Number Ten shirt but he scores goals like a Number Nine. I've watched him in Paris and his movement is brilliant.'

Zlatan couldn't believe it when he heard – his childhood hero had watched him play and he thought he was now the best striker in the world. It was a very proud moment, one that he shared with his dad.

'Do you remember when I used to have his posters on my wall?' Zlatan laughed.

'How could I forget? For years, Ronaldo was all you talked about!' Šefik replied.

Zlatan had scored twenty goals in his first twenty league games for PSG. With him up front, the team was getting better and better. In January 2013, they signed another world-class player with lots of experience.

'I think you're even more famous than me!' Zlatan joked with David Beckham on his first day.

He liked David's style and he was brilliant at crossing the ball from the right wing. It would be good to have another player at the club who had won lots of big trophies. If PSG could keep winning games, the Ligue 1 title would be theirs. Zlatan was doing his best to keep them on track. But when they lost to Sochaux, he wasn't happy at all.

'That was a disaster!' he told his teammates in the dressing room. 'If we play like that against Marseille next week, they'll win the game and the league. We can't let this slip!'

All of the players were really fired up for the Marseille match. PSG played really well and took the lead but they couldn't score a second. In the last ten minutes, the match was really tense. Could Marseille score an equaliser? The goalkeeper made lots of great saves but PSG needed another goal to make the victory safe.

Jérémy did well on the left and Zlatan was in the six-yard box waiting for his pass. At the last second, a defender rushed back to block him but Zlatan used his strength to hold him off and hit the ball into the net with his knee.

'We've won!' David shouted happily as he jumped up into Zlatan's arms.

The next big challenge was the Champions League. In the quarter-finals, PSG played Zlatan's old club Barcelona. It would be really difficult to win but Zlatan was desperate for revenge.

'When we play really well, we can beat anyone!' he told his teammates as they got ready for the big match. He was worried that some of the other players would be scared of Messi, Xavi and Iniesta. 'We have to be fearless!'

The first leg was in Paris and the atmosphere was brilliant. Barcelona scored first just before half-time but Zlatan told his teammates to keep going. 'It's not over yet!' he said again and again.

With ten minutes to go, Maxwell curled a free-kick into the penalty area. Thiago Silva's header was really powerful but it hit the post. There were lots of Barcelona defenders around the goal but Zlatan got there first to make it 1–1.

'Come on!' he shouted. He was so happy to score against the team that had let him leave.

Xavi scored a late penalty to make it 2–1 but with seconds to go, a long ball came towards Zlatan in the penalty area. He headed the ball down perfectly to Blaise and he shot past the goalkeeper. The PSG fans went wild. Thanks to Zlatan, they still had a chance to make it to the semi-finals. In the second leg, the score was 1–1 and PSG lost on the away goals rule. It was a very disappointing way to lose but Zlatan was still proud of the way his team had battled against the best team in the world.

'You guys were all amazing,' he said after the final whistle. The players were all sitting in silence in the dressing room. 'Don't worry, we'll be back next year and we'll be even better. But now, we have to move on. We've got a league title to win!'

With four more wins, PSG would become Champions of France. They won their next three matches but drew with Valenciennes. They would need to beat title challengers Lyon to win the league but Zlatan wasn't worried. There was no way that he would let his team lose.

'If I have a son, I'll call him Zlatan,' Thiago Silva told him as they prepared for their biggest game of the season. 'No-one fights for victory like you.'

Before kick-off, the players looked very nervous. It was the biggest game of their lives. Ancelotti looked nervous too. Zlatan decided that he needed to lift the pressure. It was time to show that he was a leader.

'Do you believe in me?' he asked his manager in front of the whole team.

'Of course,' Ancelotti replied.

'Then you can relax!' Zlatan said. 'We will win this title, I promise.'

After that, everyone looked a little calmer. Zlatan had enough self-belief for the whole PSG squad.

The Lyon fans waved their red, white and blue flags and cheered their team on. They really didn't want their rivals PSG to win the league in their stadium. It was a very close game and Zlatan had a shot stopped on the goal-line by a defender.

'Keep going!' he shouted to his teammates.

In the second half, Zlatan seized his chance, with the help of Thiago Motta. His clever movement and perfectly-timed run fooled the defenders into giving Jérémy space, and his teammate slotted the ball past the keeper and into the net.

Goooooooooaaaaaaaaaaaaaaaaaaalllllllllllllll lll!!!!!!!!!!!!!

Zlatan was thrilled that his plan had created the chance for one of his teammates to score on the biggest day of them all. A league-winning goal was great, and to have made the assist for it was even better.

There was a huge sense of relief and the PSG players all hugged each other. They were just thirty minutes away from the title. At the final whistle, they jumped for joy. The whole team joined together and danced around the pitch, and donned their 'Paris are Champions' T-shirts.

It was an unforgettable day but the celebrations were even bigger back in Paris a few days later. There were fireworks in the Parc des Princes Stadium and all of the players held their winner's medals above their heads. When Thiago Silva lifted the trophy, the stadium shook with the noise from the supporters. After nineteen years, PSG were the French league champions once again. They had trusted Zlatan and he hadn't let them down.

Zlatan! Zlatan! Zlatan!

Zlatan took his sons Maxi and Vincent on a lap of honour around the pitch. They were proudly wearing PSG shirts with 'Ibrahimović' on the back and the fans loved it.

It had been another great season for Zlatan. As well as winning the league, he was the top scorer in France and the Ligue 1 Player of the Year too. The boy from Rosengård was a born winner. Against the odds, Zlatan had risen from street football in Sweden to become one of the best players in the world.

'Look at me now!' he thought to himself.

Through hard work and discipline, he had gone from a skilful show-off to a top goalscorer and champion. His fairy-tale dream had come true. He owed a lot to the people who had believed in him – the scouts, the managers, the fans, the teammates, but especially Mino, his dad and Helena.

'Thank you! Thank you!' he shouted, blowing kisses into the air.

The Champions League would have to wait for another year; for now, Zlatan was just enjoying his amazing success.

CHAPTER 24

MANCHESTER CALLING

'I've got a couple of years left in my career and I want one last challenge,' Zlatan told Mino near the end of the 2015-16 season.

PSG had won the Ligue 1 title for the fourth year in a row. With one match left, Zlatan had scored an amazing 36 goals in just 30 league games. With his best season ever, he had achieved everything possible in French football.

'Ok, how do you feel about England?' Mino asked. 'There are strong rumours that Jose Mourinho will become the next Manchester United manager...'

Zlatan's smile got bigger and bigger. 'I like the sound of that!' Of all the managers that he had worked with, Jose was definitely the best. At Inter Milan, they were unstoppable. Together, they could get Manchester United back to the top.

'I came like a king, I leave like a legend, but I will be back,' Zlatan told the PSG fans on Twitter. Like his hero Muhammad Ali, he loved to 'talk the talk' *and* 'walk the walk'.

It was a very emotional goodbye. After ten minutes of his final match, the game stopped and all of the supporters stood up and clapped their amazing Number 10. Many of them were even wearing masks with his face on. Zlatan had goosebumps as he looked up into the stands. He would really miss the club.

Zlatan scored two more goals to make it 38 for the season. What a record! At the final whistle, Maxi and Vincent ran on to lead him off the pitch. They had 'King' and Legend' written on the back of their shirts. It was a perfect way to go.

It wasn't long before Mourinho got in touch. 'Zlatan, this is your chance to play in the best league in the world for the best club in the world,' the new Manchester United manager told him. 'We've got some great young players but we need a big superstar with lots of experience. That's you!'

Zlatan knew all about the club's history, and Wayne Rooney and the new stars Anthony Martial and Marcus Rashford. After finishing fifth last season, Manchester United needed to challenge for the title again. That was Jose's big challenge and Zlatan knew it was exactly the exciting project that he was looking for. Having played in the top leagues in Holland, Italy, Spain and France, he was desperate to play in the English Premier League.

'Let's make this happen!' he told Mino.

After a disappointing Euro 2016 in France, Zlatan retired from playing for the Swedish national team. He had worked so hard for his country for many years and he was proud of his record – 62 goals in 116 matches. There were so many great memories, especially those four brilliant goals against England. But he was thirty-four years old now. If he wanted to play for another few years, Zlatan needed to be careful.

At the start of July, everything was agreed. 'My next destination is Manchester United', Zlatan told the world through Twitter.

'I can't wait for this new and exciting challenge,' he told the English media, as he held up the club shirt with his name on the back. Wayne was the Number '10' and so Zlatan took '9', the classic number for a top, goalscoring striker.

Some critics in the newspapers said that he was too old and slow for the Premier League but Zlatan was determined to prove them wrong yet again. He had come to Old Trafford to score lots more goals and win lots more trophies. He worked harder than ever in pre-season training and his new teammates were very impressed.

'Wow, he's so professional,' Marcus said to Jesse Lingard. 'He's even got his own physio!'

'I'm never seen anyone who wants to win so much!' Jesse replied.

Zlatan loved to give the young players lots of advice. If they could share his focus and confidence, he was sure that they could win the Premier League title.

In a friendly against Galatasaray, Zlatan made his first appearance for Manchester United alongside Wayne and Anthony in attack. He was raring to go.

After four minutes, Antonio Valencia made a run down the right wing. Zlatan had three defenders around him in the penalty area but he was ready for the cross. It was slightly behind him but that wasn't a problem for Zlatan. Just as he had so many times before, he jumped into the air for a scissor-kick. The ball flew into the back of the net.

Goooooooooooooooooooooooaaaaaaaaaaaaallllllllllllll llllllll!!!!!!!!!!!!!!!!!!

The other players ran to celebrate with him. On the bench, Mourinho nearly smiled. What a start to his Manchester United career. Zlatan couldn't wait for the Premier League season to start.

ZLATAN IBRAHIMOVIĆ HONOURS

Ajax

- ★ Eredivisie (Dutch league): 2001–02, 2003–04
- ★ KNVB Cup: 2001–02

Juventus

- ★ Serie A: 2004–05, 2005–06

Inter Milan

- ★ Serie A: 2006–07, 2007–08, 2008–09

Barcelona

- ★ La Liga: 2009–10
- ★ FIFA Club World Cup: 2009

AC Milan
★ Serie A: 2010–11

Paris Saint-Germain
★ Ligue 1: 2012–13, 2013–14, 2014–15, 2015–16
★ Coupe de France: 2014–15
★ Coupe de la Ligue: 2013–14, 2014–15, 2015–16

Individual
★ Guldbollen (Swedish Footballer of the Year): 2005, 2007, 2008, 2009, 2010, 2011, 2012, 2013, 2014, 2015
★ Serie A Foreign Footballer of the Year: 2005, 2008, 2009
★ UEFA Team of the Year: 2007, 2009, 2013, 2014
★ Serie A Footballer of the Year: 2008, 2009, 2011
★ Serie A Top Scorer: 2009, 2012
★ Ligue 1 Player of the Year: 2012–13, 2013–14, 2014–15, 2015–16
★ Ligue 1 Top Goalscorer: 2012–13, 2013–14, 2015–16

★ FIFA Puskás Award for Best Goal of the Year: 2013
★ UEFA Champions League Team of the Season: 2013–14

Turn the page for a sneak preview of
another brilliant football story by
Matt and Tom Oldfield. . .

WAYNE ROONEY
CAPTAIN OF ENGLAND

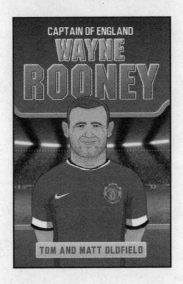

Available now!

978 1 78418 647 0

CHAPTER 1

OLD TRAFFORD'S NEW HERO

'Roo-ney! Roo-ney! Roo-ney!'

It was the sound of 75,000 fans chanting his name. Wayne just stared straight ahead down the tunnel. His heart was beating fast – in fact, it had been pounding since he put on the famous red Manchester United shirt in the dressing room ten minutes earlier. It was a long time since he had felt this nervous about playing football. But then this wasn't just any game.

It was 28 September 2004 and he was just minutes away from the start of his United career. Where was the referee? 'Come on, let's go,' he muttered to himself.

Tonight's game against Turkish giants Fenerbahce in the Champions League was the start of a new chapter for Wayne. He was following in the footsteps of George Best, Bobby Charlton, Eric Cantona, Bryan Robson and so many other United legends. Now Wayne would have the chance to add his name to that list.

As he thought about his whirlwind journey from the streets of Croxteth in Liverpool to the Theatre of Dreams, Wayne smiled to himself. He had started his first Premier League game for Everton just two years ago and now he was about to make his debut for one of the biggest clubs in the world. The hairs on his neck stood on end.

A broken bone in his foot had delayed his debut and United had begun the new season without him. But all anyone wanted to know was when Wayne would be back. When would United fans get their first glimpse of the teenage sensation who had cost £30 million that summer? And how would he top his incredible performances at Euro 2004?

Wayne wanted to make up for lost time. His foot had been fine in training this week and he just hoped that there would be no pain once he put it to the test in a real game.

As crowds of United fans walked down Sir Matt Busby Way that night, there was a different buzz in the air. Wayne would be making his debut and they were going to share in that experience. Many of them already had 'Rooney' on the back of their United shirts.

Just before the teams walked out onto the pitch, Ryan Giggs walked up to Wayne and patted him on the back. Maybe he could sense Wayne's nerves. 'Don't put too much pressure on yourself tonight. Just enjoy it – you only get to make your Manchester United debut once!'

He winked then shook Wayne's hand. 'The club's going to be in your hands some day soon. This is where it all begins for you.'

Finally, the waiting was over. He took a deep breath and stretched his neck to one side and then the other. Showtime.

As he walked across the Old Trafford turf, the Champions League anthem blared out and caught

Wayne by surprise. It was the first time he had heard it for one of his games. It always gave him goosebumps when he heard it on television but it was a hundred times better in person. That's why I had to make this move, he reminded himself.

As he jumped up and down and did some final stretches, he spotted his family in the crowd among the sea of red shirts. His fiancée, Colleen, was there with them. They were waving and cheering. The last two months had been difficult for the whole family and he was happy that they were with him tonight as he put on the United shirt for the first time.

Wayne's decision to leave Everton had shaken the blue half of the city. He had been called Judas, a traitor and a greedy kid. Wayne would always love Everton. They had believed in him and given him a chance to shine. But he just had to take this next step.

The crowd was so noisy that Wayne didn't hear Sir Alex Ferguson at first. Eventually, he realised his manager was on the touchline and wanted a final word with him. He ran over. 'You were born to play on this stage, Wayne,' Ferguson said. 'Give these defenders the worst night of their lives. The fans want to see something special, so give them a show to remember.'

The football pitch was always where Wayne felt most at home. As he walked into the centre circle for the kick-off with new strike partner Ruud van Nistelrooy, the nerves were replaced with excitement. After all, football had been part of his life from the very start.

COLLECT THEM ALL

SERGIO AGÜERO
THE LITTLE GENIUS

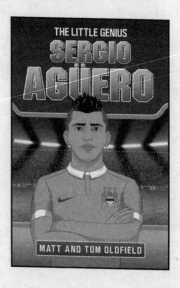

The Little Genius is the tale of the boy who would go on to re-write football history forever. His dramatic 94th minute goal on the final day of the 2012/13 season, to snatch the title from under rivals Manchester United's noses, was the most electric moment in Premier League history. This is how the small boy from Argentina became the biggest hero of all.

978 1 78606 218 5

£5.99

COLLECT THEM ALL

STEVEN GERRARD
CAPTAIN FANTASTIC

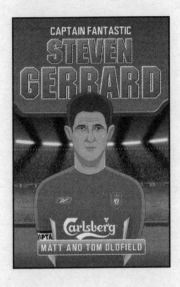

Steven Gerrard: Captain Fantastic tells of how a young boy from
Merseyside overcame personal tragedy in the Hillsborough disaster
to make his dream of playing for Liverpool FC come true. But that
boy was no ordinary footballer; he would go on to captain his club
for over a decade, inspiring their legendary Champions League
FA Cup wins along the way. This is the story of Steven Gerrard,
Liverpool's greatest ever player.

978 1 78606 219 2
£5.99

COLLECT THEM ALL

ALEXIS SÁNCHEZ
THE WONDER BOY

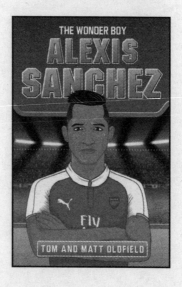

Alexis Sánchez: The Wonder Boy tells the story of the Arsenal superstar's incredible journey from the streets of Tocopilla to become 'The Boy Wonder', a national hero, and one of the most talented players in the world. With his pace, skill and eye for a goal, Alexis is now one of the Premier League's biggest stars. The story is every bit as exciting as the player.

978 1 78606 013 6

£5.99

COLLECT THEM ALL

LUIS SUAREZ
EL PISTOLERO

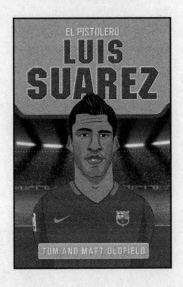

Luis Suárez: El Pistolero follows the Uruguayan's winding path
from love-struck youngster to Liverpool hero to Barcelona star.
Grabbing goals and headlines along the way, Luis chased his
dreams and became a Champions League winner. This is
the inspiring story of how the world's deadliest striker
made his mark.

978 1 786060129

£5.99

COLLECT THEM ALL

EDEN HAZARD
THE BOY IN BLUE

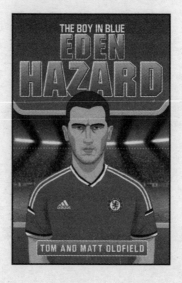

Eden Hazard: The Boy in Blue is the thrilling tale of how the
wing wizard went from local wonder kid to league champion.
With the support of his football-obsessed family, Eden worked
hard to develop his amazing dribbling skills and earn his
dream transfer to Chelsea.

978 1 78606 014 3
£5.99

COLLECT THEM ALL

GARETH BALE
THE BOY WHO BECAME A GALÁCTICO

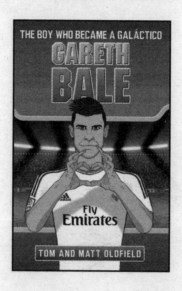

Gareth Bale: The Boy Who Became a Galáctico tracks the Welsh wizard's impressive rise from talented schoolboy to Real Madrid star. This is the inspiring story of how Bale beat the odds and became the most expensive player in football history.

978 1 78418 645 7

£5.99

COLLECT THEM ALL

WAYNE ROONEY
CAPTAIN OF ENGLAND

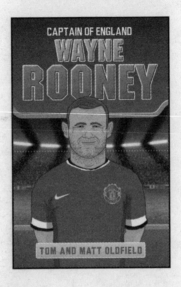

Wayne Rooney: Captain of England tells the action-packed story of one boy's journey from the streets of Croxteth to one of the biggest stages in world football. This heartwarming book tracks Rooney's fairytale rise from child superstar to Everton hero to Manchester United legend.

978 1 78418 647 0

£5.99